The Best and Worst Baseball Teams Of All Time

Harry Hollingsworth

SPi BOOKS

A Division Of Shapolsky Publishers

The Best And Worst Baseball Teams Of All Time

S.P.I. BOOKS
A division of Shapolsky Publishers, Inc.

Copyright © 1994 by Harry Hollingsworth

ISBN 1-56171-308-2

For any additional information, contact:

S.P.I. BOOKS/Shapolsky Publishers, Inc.
136 West 22nd Street
New York, NY 10011
212/633-2022 / FAX 212/633-2123

Manufactured in Canada

10 9 8 7 6 5 4 3 2 1

Contents

Chapter 12

Chapter 14

Chapter 15

Chapter 16

Chapter 22

PART III
TRENDS IN THE
BEST AND WORST

Chapter 23

ACKNOWLEDGEMENTS

First, I would like to acknowledge the all-round assistance of my son, Howard, without which I could not have completed this book.

My thanks also to my friend, Ralph Ranney, and my sister, Mary Shaw, for their help in developing sources and in research.

Also, to my friend, Dr. Alan Clive, for his encouragement and suggestions.

Finally, to my wife, Betty, for her expert copyreading and support during the project.

H. H. H.

Chapter 1
Introduction

The purpose of this book is to fill what we believe is a glaring gap in the massive and ever growing literature of baseball.

Which were the greatest baseball teams of all time? Which were the worst?

How do some of the great teams of recent years compare with the great old teams? How, for example, do the 1988 Oakland Athletics rank among the great teams of all time? How about the 1986 New York Mets? The 1984 Detroit Tigers? The 1975 and 1976 Cincinnati Reds? The 1969 and 1970 Baltimore Orioles? The 1961 New York Yankees?

Among the worst, how do some recent teams rank? How about those expansion teams including New York, Houston, San Diego, or more recently, Colorado and Florida?

We checked the public libraries, the Baseball Hall of Fame at Cooperstown and the reference service at the *Sporting News* and turned up only three books, one booklet and one article on the subject of the best teams. Only one, Harold Siner's book, *Sweet Seasons: Baseball's Greatest Teams*, published in 1988, lists as many as 25 teams. *Sports Illustrated's* booklet, *Baseball's 20 Greatest Teams of All Time*, published in 1991, lists 20. Donald Honig's book, *Baseball's Ten Greatest Teams*, published in 1982, lists only 10 teams and does not put them in order except for naming the best of all time. Nate

Aaseng, in his 1986 book, *Baseball's Greatest Teams*, lists just eight teams in order. George Vass, in his article, "Baseball's All-time Greatest Teams," in *Baseball Digest* of September, 1974, also lists just eight teams. (In Table 18, we show how these experts ranked the top teams compared with how our computer ranked them.)

The picture is similar on the worst teams. (We discuss the sources available later.)

None of these studies employs a statistical approach to evaluating the teams, despite the abundance of data available; and no one has used the computer to do so. Volumes of material have been produced on every other sort of qualitiative analysis of some aspect of baseball. But none on the teams, without them there would be no baseball.

And to this end, we put our computer to work determining the 30 best and 30 worst teams of all time. Our principal statistical source was *The Baseball Encyclopedia* (Macmillan).

A second purpose of the book is to describe the players on the great teams as described by contemporary sources, including many sportswriters. It is interesting to learn what writers at the time thought of these teams and their players, and to read the flowery sports lingo once used on the sports pages of America's newspapers.

PART I
THE BEST TEAMS

Chapter 2
How We Selected the Best Teams

In selecting the best teams, the questions that first needed to be answered were:

1. Should all former major league teams be considered, or just pennant winners and just during the "modern era?"

2. What statistical measures or criteria should be used?

What Teams and What Period?

We decided that only pennant winners should be considered (even though it was possible that a team that finished second in one year was better than one that finished first in another).

Second, we decided that because the rules of baseball were so different before 1901, only teams that played in 1901 and later should be considered.

As a result, we analyzed 186 teams that won league pennants between 1901 and 1993.

Baseball was really a different game prior to 1900. Until 1881, pitchers stood only 45 feet from home plate. Between 1881 and 1893, they stood only 50 feet away. Foul tips were not counted as strikes until 1895. In 1900, the size of home plate was enlarged. In 1901, for the first time foul balls were counted as strikes.

In the sports pages of the *New York Times* of Feb. 28, 1901, we read that the American League had been organized and a new rule adopted: "Hereafter, the catcher must play up close to the bat at all times, the position to be within 10 feet of the batter," (instead of a range of 90 feet).

In the 19th century, many pitchers pitched underhand and could pitch almost as often as softball pitchers do today.

There have been some significant trends and changes in baseball since 1901, but none compares with the changes that took place before the start of this century.

The Criteria Used

Defining "Best." Before discussing the specific criteria we decided to employ in this study, we need to define precisely what we mean by the "best" team.

Would the "best" team be (1) one which would be expected to defeat any other pennant-winning team if it were possible to conduct a series between them today in a neutral ball park?

Or, is the "best" team (2) the best in terms of its superiority over teams playing at the same time, as compared with the superiority of other teams over their competition in other eras?

In other words, would the 1927 New York Yankees, which we've determined to be the best team of all time (as do most studies), be able to defeat teams playing 50 and 60 years later, even though the later teams have athletes who are bigger, stronger, faster, healthier and better equipped, trained and coached?

Or, are the 1927 Yankees the best simply because they were so far ahead of the teams of their era, more so than any other team was ahead of teams in its era (even though some other team might actually be able to beat the 1927 Yankees if the game were played in a neutral ball park today)?

Using this second definition in a different sport, for

example, we could call Roger Bannister, the first man to run the four-minute mile, "the greatest miler of all time," even though literally hundreds of milers have run the mile in a faster time since.

Actually, this is a moot question for all practical purposes, for there is no way to compare teams quantitatively using the first definition. The only way the best team can be determined using this definition is judgmentally, with very little to go on beyond what we determine using definition 2.

So, it is definition 2 that we use when we define "best."

Nevertheless, it is possible that the best team determined using this definition is also the best using definition 1. In fact, in the case of the '27 Yanks, it is likely. However, it is not as likely that the teams from the early part of the century which outrank more recent teams could actually beat them on the playing field.

Selecting the Criteria. We selected the criteria by considering all data available since 1901. It was possible to use statistical measures to reject certain ones (e.g., fielding average and stolen bases - see later discussion), but it was necessary to use judgment in the final selection of the criteria and their weights. There is no independent variable against which Percentage of Games Won or Games Ahead of Second can be measured.

Eleven Criteria. Eleven different statistical measures or criteria were used. They divide into three categories:
* Three general measures
* Six offensive measures
* Two defensive measures.

Adjusting Measures To Make Them Comparable. In developing the measures to be used, we ran into the fact that the number of games played in various eras differed, giving teams that played the longer schedules more chances to make hits, runs, etc.

Thus, teams that played in years when only 140 or 154 games were scheduled would be at a disadvantage on certain measures such as runs scored. As a result, we "normalized" all data to a 154-game schedule. That is, we reduced the measure by multiplying it by 154/162 or 95% in the years since expansion, and increased it by multiplying it by 154/140 or 110% in the early years when only 140 games were scheduled.

Making Measures Comparable Over Time. In developing our offensive and defensive criteria, we also observed the fact that baseball has changed significantly over the years since 1901, which has had a large effect on a number of statistical measures. This can be seen in the following table:

Table 1
How Baseball Has Changed
(Averages for All Teams in Both Leagues During Decade)

YEARS	Batting	Home Runs*	ERA	Slugging
1901-1910	.252	21	2.81	.326
1911-1920	.258	27	3.01	.341
1921-1930	.287	68	4.17	.403
1931-1940	.276	84	4.21	.395
1941-1950	.260	84	3.78	.369
1951-1960	.258	131	3.92	.390
1961-1970	.249	125	3.58	.374
1971-1980	.257	112	3.68	.376
1981-1990	.258	123	3.84	.386

* - Adjusted to 154-game schedule.

As the foregoing table shows, years prior to 1920 in the dead ball era, there were very few home runs and both slugging averages and earned run averages were lower.

In the first decade, only 21 home runs were hit per team per season. In the twenties, led by the great Yankee teams, the average jumped to 68 per year. In the thirties, it was up to 84. In the fifties, it was up to 131 and it has been close to that level since.

Also note how the average ERA jumped to 4.17 in the twenties and reached an all-time high in the thirties.

What are the reasons for these differences?

In addition to the more lively ball, night baseball was introduced in the late thirties. Artificial surfaces were introduced in the late sixties. Then came bigger ball parks, much larger gloves and mitts, and the development of a lot of new pitches. The slider was introduced after World War II and more recently the very effective split finger fast ball came in.

Also, there has been a revolution in how and when pitchers are utilized, with far greater emphasis placed on relievers and "closers" the last few decades.

For example, the 1991 New York Yankee starting pitchers completed only three games. In the early years of this century, even the very worst teams had 50 or more complete games.

To cope with these variations, we have used a "net" concept for many of our criteria. With runs, for example, this involved subtracting the average number of runs scored by all the teams in its given league that year from the number of runs scored by the team in question. This gives the "net runs" and thus tells how much better the team is in this category than the average team playing under the same conditions that year.

Still another reason for the need for this net concept is the fact that the American League uses the designated hitter. As a result, AL team batting averages and earned run averages tend to be higher.

General Measures

The general measures and the weight given to each are:

1. Percentage of games won - 25%

2. Games ahead of the second place team in the team's league or division after division play started in 1969 - 15%.

3. World Series Net (games won minus games lost in the World Series) - 5%.

These general measures thus account for 45%. Keep in mind that the total for all 11 measures will be 100%.

The reason Percentage of Games Won is given a relatively high weight (25%) is that it best measures winning, the purpose of the game. The higher the percentage, other things being equal, the better the team. The problem is that other things often are not equal. A team may be playing in an era of weak teams or strong teams. So, other criteria are also needed.

Games Ahead of Second is a measure of how strong the team is compared with the next strongest team in the league. The great teams tend to outdistance their runner-ups by greater margins.

Top teams also tend to perform well in the World Series and that is the reason for using World Series Net. We give it no more weight than 5% because a four to seven game series is not a broad enough base to give a lot of weight. How the ball bounces often determines whether a team sweeps or wins four of seven.

Offensive Measures

Here are the offensive criteria and the weight assigned to each:

4. Runs scored - 5%

5. Net runs scored - 5%

6. Batting average - 5%

7. Net batting average - 5%
8. Net slugging average - 5%
9. Net home runs - 5%

All these offensive measures tend to correlate highly with each other. We think there are some advantages to looking at offense in a number of different ways.

The unadjusted measures - runs, batting average and earned run average - are affected by the change in the nature of the game through the years. However, when batting averages were down, so were earned run averages, and when they went up, so did earned run averages. Runs did not have a similar balancing factor, but scoring them is one of the main purposes of the game and it seemed fair to include them with a 5% weight.

The net measures are not affected by the changes in the nature of the game.

Team speed, as reflected in stolen bases, was not included. The reason will be explained later.

Defensive Measures

The defensive measures are:

10. Earned run average - 5%
11. Net earned run average - 20%

Fielding, as reflected in the fielding average, was not included, for reasons explained below.

Earned run average is considered to be the best measure of pitching, which in turn is critical to a team's success. We look at ERA two ways.

Why Not Fielding and Speed?

Even though good fielding and speed obviously can be great assets to a team, statistical analysis shows that fielding average, itself, and the number of stolen bases, have little effect in determining a team's number of wins.[1]

In our analysis, we determined how well four factors were able to explain the percentage of games won by each team. The four factors were team slugging average, team earned run average, team fielding percentage, and team stolen bases.

Slugging average is the best single measure of offensive power, covering not only hits but also extra base hits, and thus can be considered to represent all the "offensive" measures we used.

Earned run average is the best single measure of pitching, which not incidentally, most experts consider the most important determinant of a team's success. Thus, it represents our defensive measures.

As already reported, we made five analyses, one covering all data for all four years and one each for each of the individual years. All five analyses gave the same result: fielding average and stolen bases have little bearing on the percentage of games won by a team.

The four factors together explained from 85% to 94% of the variation in the dependent variable, the percentage of games won. Virtually all of this was explained by just two of the variables: slugging average and earned run average.

Looking at the four years combined, 85% of the total variation was explained by the four factors in combination. However, if we drop fielding average as one of the

1. We selected a sample of four representative years to make a statistical analysis: 1930, 1940, 1950 and 1960. It should be noted that 1960 was the last year before expansion, so we had 16 teams to analyze each year. We looked at the data both in total for the four years, and in each year separately.

factors, we find that it accounts for less than 1% of the variation. Stolen bases account for even less. Thus, 85% of the total variation was explained by the four factors combined, but 84% was explained by just slugging average and earned run average.

And the same thing was true looking at each year separately. For 1930, fielding average and stolen bases each accounted for less than 1%. For 1940, fielding average explained less than 1% but stolen bases accounted for 5%. For 1950, both accounted for less than 1%. For 1960, fielding accounted for 4% and stolen bases for 2%.

The analysis suggests that a team wins one extra game for each 32 bases it steals and loses an additional game for every 11 errors it commits.

In another check of fielding average, we took a sample of 34 years and found that in four, the pennant winner had a lower fielding average than the league as a whole. In four others, it had the same fielding average as the league. And in 11 more years, its fielding average was only .001 to .002 points better than the league's.

This also suggests that fielding average has little bearing on what team wins the pennant, and therefore, on which are the best and worst teams.

The problem with fielding average seems to be that it is not a completely accurate measure of how good a team is at fielding. This must be determined not only by lack of errors, but, more importantly, by how much ground the fielders cover.

(A member of the Statistical Committee of the Society for American Baseball Research (SABR) recently suggested that such a measure could be determined by calculating what percentage of all balls put in play by the opponents result in assists and putouts.)

Chapter 3
The 10 Best Teams by Criterion

In understanding why certain teams were outstanding and others were not, it is helpful to look at the best teams by each of the 11 criteria we used. In going through these tables, notice how often certain teams appear.

Percentage of Games Won

Table 2
Percentage of Games Won (25%)

1.1906 Chicago Cubs .763
2.1902 Pittsburgh Pirates .741
3.1909 Pittsburgh Pirates .724
4.1954 Cleveland Indians .721
5.1927 New York Yankees .714
6.1931 Philadelphia Athletics .704
6.1907 Chicago Cubs .704
8.1939 New York Yankees .702
9.1932 New York Yankees .695
10.1904 New York Giants .693
10.1929 Philadelphia Athletics .693

The 1906 Chicago Cubs set the all-time record by winning more than three-fourths of their games. Their ratio was .763.

Note how few of these teams played after World War II. We later discuss this trend to parity in baseball.

Games Ahead of Second

Table 3
Games Ahead of Second Place (15%)

1. 1902 Pittsburgh Pirates 27.5
2. 1986 New York Mets 21.5
3. 1975 Cincinnati Reds 20
3. 1906 Chicago Cubs 20
5. 1936 New York Yankees 19.5
6. 1969 Baltimore Orioles 19
6. 1927 New York Yankees 19
8. 1929 Philadelphia Athletics 18
8. 1943 St. Louis Cardinals 18
10. 1907 Chicago Cubs 17
10. 1939 New York Yankees 17
10. 1941 New York Yankees 17

Here are the 1902 Pirates again, this time finishing 27 1/2 games ahead of the second place National League team. Keep in mind that they were also second in percentage of games won.

The 1986 New York Mets were second with a 21 1/2-game margin.

World Series Net

Table 4
Games Won Less Games Lost in World Series (5%)

1. 1907 Chicago Cubs +4
1. 1914 Boston Braves +4
1. 1922 New York Giants +4
1. 1927 New York Yankees +4
1. 1928 New York Yankees +4
1. 1932 New York Yankees +4
1. 1938 New York Yankees +4
1. 1939 New York Yankees +4
1. 1950 New York Yankees +4
1. 1954 New York Giants +4

1. 1963 Los Angeles Dodgers +4
1. 1966 Baltimore Orioles +4
1. 1976 Cincinnati Reds +4
1. 1989 Oakland Athletics +4
1. 1990 Cincinnati Reds +4

Fifteen teams tied for first in World Series Net by sweeping their series. This includes six Yankee teams.

Runs

Table 5
Runs (5%)

1. 1936 New York Yankees 1,065
2. 1930 St. Louis Cardinals 1,004
3. 1932 New York Yankees 1,002
4. 1929 Chicago Cubs 982
5. 1937 New York Yankees 979
6. 1927 New York Yankees 975
7. 1939 New York Yankees 967
8. 1938 New York Yankees 966
9. 1934 Detroit Tigers 958
10. 1953 Brooklyn Dodgers 955

The 1936 Yankees scored more runs than any other team.

Net Runs

Table 6
Net Runs (5%)

1. 1902 Pittsburgh Pirates +242
2. 1953 Brooklyn Dodgers +216
3. 1927 New York Yankees +213
4. 1976 Cincinnati Reds +202
5. 1932 New York Yankees +197
6. 1913 Philadelphia Athletics +191
7. 1936 New York Yankees +189
8. 1949 Brooklyn Dodgers +173
8. 1914 Philadelphia Athletics +173
10. 1934 Detroit Tigers +170

The 1902 Pirates were first, scoring 242 more runs than the average team in the NL that year. The 1927 New York Yankees were third (there they are again).

Batting Average

Table 7
Batting Average (5%)

1. 1930 St. Louis Cardinals .314
2. 1925 Pittsburgh Pirates .307
2. 1927 New York Yankees .307
4. 1927 Pittsburgh Pirates .305
5. 1922 New York Giants .304
6. 1920 Cleveland Indians .303
6. 1929 Chicago Cubs .303
6. 1925 Washington Nationals (later Senators) .303
9. 1936 New York Yankees .300
9. 1934 Detroit Tigers .300
9. 1921 New York Yankees .300
9. 1924 New York Giants .300

The 1930 St. Louis Cardinals had the highest batting average, .314. The 1925 Pirates and the 1927 Yanks were tied for second.

Net Batting Average

Table 8
Net Batting Average (x1,000) (5%)

1. 1902 Pittsburgh Pirates +27
2. 1976 Cincinnati Reds +25
2. 1908 Detroit Tigers +25
4. 1914 Philadelphia Athletics +24
4. 1913 Philadelphia Athletics +24
6. 1911 Philadelphia Athletics +23
6. 1927 Pittsburgh Pirates +23
6. 1910 Philadelphia Athletics +23

6. 1909 Detroit Tigers +23
10. 1927 New York Yankees +22
10. 1971 Pittsburgh Pirates +22

The 1902 Pirates were first, 27 points (actually .027) above the average for all National League teams in 1902. The 1927 Yankees were tenth in this category.

Net Slugging Average

Table 9
Net Slugging Average (x1,000) (5%)

1. 1927 New York Yankees +90
2. 1953 Brooklyn Dodgers +63
2. 1976 Cincinnati Reds +63
4. 1936 New York Yankees +62
5. 1921 New York Yankees +56
6. 1902 Pittsburgh Pirates +55
7. 1928 New York Yankees +53
7. 1982 Milwaukee Brewers +53
9. 1932 New York Yankees +50
9. 1971 Pittsburgh Pirates +50

The 1927 Yankees were the greatest sluggers of all time, a full 90 points higher than the average team in the AL in 1927. Tied for second are the 1953 Dodgers and the 1976 Reds, fourth are the 1936 Yanks and fifth, the 1921 Yanks. Here again, are the 1927 Yanks and three of the top five are Yankee teams.

Net Home Runs

Table 10
Net Home Runs (5%)

1.	1927 New York Yankees	+103
2.	1936 New York Yankees	+87
2.	1963 New York Yankees	+87
4.	1961 New York Yankees	+83
5.	1921 New York Yankees	+74
6.	1937 New York Yankees	+73
6.	1928 New York Yankees	+73
8.	1932 New York Yankees	+71
8.	1968 Detroit Tigers	+71
10.	1926 New York Yankees	+68

Here yet again are the 1927 Bronx Bombers, the top team in net homers, hitting a remarkable 103 more than the average team in the AL that year! Bear in mind that during the first two decades of the twentieth century, the average Big League team hit only 24 home runs per season, and even in the twenties when the Yankees were riding high, the average team was hitting only 68.

The 1927 Yanks were led by the immortal Babe Ruth who hit 60 home runs, a single season record that stood for 34 years, until Roger Maris hit 61 in a season eight games longer. (If we "normalized" these feats, Ruth would still have the record.)

In second place were the 1936 Yankees, without Ruth but with a rookie named Joe DiMaggio. Roger Maris played for the 1963 Yankees who tied for second and set the home run record while playing for the 1961 Yankees who are fourth.

The 1921 Yanks were fifth and the 1928 Yanks, sixth.

Yankee teams clearly dominate this category, taking the first eight positions.

Earned Run Average

Table 11
Earned Run Average (5%)

1. 1907 Chicago Cubs 1.73
2. 1906 Chicago Cubs 1.76
3. 1910 Philadelphia Athletics 1.78
4. 1909 Pittsburgh Pirates 2.07
5. 1916 Brooklyn Robins (later Dodgers) 2.12
5. 1904 Boston Pilgrims (now Red Sox) 2.12
7. 1906 Chicago White Sox 2.13
8. 1908 Chicago Cubs 2.14
9. 1917 Chicago White Sox 2.16
10. 1904 New York Giants 2.17
10. 1915 Philadelphia Phillies 2.17

The 1907 Cubs were first with an ERA of 1.73.
All the teams leading in this category played before
1920—before the advent of the so called "lively ball."

Net Earned Run Average

Table 12
Net Earned Run Average (20%)

1. 1939 New York Yankees -1.31
2. 1948 Cleveland Indians -1.06
3. 1966 Los Angeles Dodgers -.99
4. 1954 New York Giants -.98
5. 1937 New York Yankees -.97
6. 1979 Baltimore Orioles -.96
7. 1944 St. Louis Cardinals -.94
7. 1954 Cleveland Indians -.94
9. 1927 New York Yankees -.92
10. 1931 Philadelphia Athletics -.91

This is a much more meaningful measure than the
unadjusted ERA and that is why it counts for four times
as much. In first place are the 1939 Yanks, with an

ERA 1.31 points lower than the average for the AL in 1939. In second are the 1948 Cleveland Indians; in third, the 1966 Los Angeles Dodgers; in fourth, the 1954 New York Giants and in fifth, the 1937 Yankees.

Not only did the Yankees field great hitting teams, but they also had outstanding pitching. Here you see the 1927 Yanks again, not only the greatest slugging team in history, but also ninth best in pitching!

Chapter 4
The Top 30 Teams of All Time

While they did not agree on anything else, recent books and articles identifying the best baseball teams of all time *did* agree on the best single team: the 1927 New York Yankees. And our computer agreed.

The top 30 teams of all time and their composite scores are:

1. 1927 New York Yankees 94.6
2. 1939 New York Yankees 90.7
3. 1929 Philadelphia Athletics 87.6
4. 1906 Chicago Cubs 86.2
5. 1902 Pittsburgh Pirates 86.0
6. 1936 New York Yankees 85.2
7. 1944 St. Louis Cardinals 84.1
8. 1931 Philadelphia Athletics 83.8
9. 1943 St. Louis Cardinals 81.8
10. 1932 New York Yankees 81.6
11. 1937 New York Yankees 80.6
12. 1969 Baltimore Orioles 79.8
13. 1910 Philadelphia Athletics 79.4
14. 1912 New York Giants 78.8
15. 1912 Boston Red Sox 78.7
16. 1954 Cleveland Indians 78.6
17. 1907 Chicago Cubs 78.5
18. 1905 New York Giants 78.4
19. 1942 St. Louis Cardinals 76.7
20. 1904 New York Giants 76.3
21. 1953 Brooklyn Dodgers 76.0
22. 1909 Pittsburgh Pirates 75.3
23. 1911 Philadelphia Athletics 75.2
24. 1986 New York Mets 74.6
25. 1942 New York Yankees 74.4
26. 1941 New York Yankees 73.7

27. 1938 New York Yankees 73.6
28. 1975 Cincinnati Reds 73.3
29. 1903 Boston Pilgrims (now Red Sox) 73.0
30. 1953 New York Yankees 73.0

In the following pages, we take a closer look at these teams. For each, we give the number of players on the team who are in the Baseball Hall of Fame in Cooperstown, New York, through 1994. We counted only Hall of Famers who had appeared in at least 100 games for the team as position players or appeared in at least 20 games as pitchers.

Incidentally, this gives us, for comparisons sake, an index of which were the best teams of all time (as shown in Table 14), as opposed to which teams might have had the greatest *personnel* of all time—regardless of on-field results.

Table 14

Pennant Winning Teams With Greatest Number of Members of Hall of Fame

Rank	Team	Number
1.	1932 Yankees	9
2.	1927 Yankees	6
2.	1928 Yankees	6
2.	1934 Cardinals	6
2.	1936 Yankees	6
2.	1937 Yankees	6
7.	1930 Cardinals	5
8.	1901 Pirates	4
8.	1906 Cubs	4
8.	1907 Cubs	4
8.	1910 Athletics	4
8.	1911 Athletics	4
8.	1922 Giants	4
8.	1929 Athletics	4
8.	1930 Athletics	4

8.	1931 Athletics	4
8.	1931 Cardinals	4
8.	1934 Tigers	4
8.	1935 Cubs	4
8.	1938 Yankees	4
8.	1939 Yankees	4
8.	1941 Yankees	4
8.	1948 Indians	4
8.	1953 Dodgers	4
8.	1955 Dodgers	4
8.	1956 Yankees	4
8.	1957 Braves	4
28.	1902 Pirates	3
28.	1904 Giants	3
28.	1910 Cubs	3
28.	1915 Red Sox	3
28.	1919 White Sox	3
28.	1923 Yankees	3
28.	1924 Nationals	3
28.	1925 Pirates	3
28.	1927 Pirates	3
28.	1929 Cubs	3
28.	1950 Yankees	3
28.	1951 Yankees	3
28.	1953 Yankees	3
28.	1954 Giants	3
28.	1954 Indians	3
28.	1957 Yankees	3
28.	1958 Yankees	3
28.	1961 Yankees	3
28.	1969 Orioles	3
28.	1970 Orioles	3
28.	1971 Orioles	3
28.	1973 Athletics	3
28.	1974 Athletics	3

Chapter 5
The Best Team of All Time:
the 1927 Yankees

Members of Hall of Fame: 6.

Surprisingly, even though they had won the American League pennant in 1926, only nine of 42 baseball writers polled before the start of the 1927 season picked the Yankees to win the American League pennant. Nineteen of them picked the Pittsburgh Pirates to win the NL pennant, which the Pirates did.

What a team this was! That year, Babe Ruth hit 60 home runs, batted .356 and drove in 164 runs. Lou Gehrig, the Yankees' great first baseman, batted .373 and hit 47 home runs. He led the league in runs batted in with 175. Center fielder Earle Combs batted .356. Second baseman Tony Lazzeri batted .309 and drove in 102 runs. Left fielder Bob Meusel hit .337 with 103 RBI.

To put Ruth's 60 home runs in perspective, consider that no other American League *team* hit as many homers in total as Ruth did all by himself that year. The Cleveland Indians had the fewest, only 26 - fewer than half Ruth's number. The Indians' home run leader was reserve third baseman, Johnny Hodapp, who hit 5!

The 1927 Yankees' domination is clearly indicated by their top ten finish in ten of the eleven categories we used to evaluate the pennant winners.

These Yanks were first in Net Slugging Average and

Net Home Runs, as well as tied for first in World Series Net. They were second in Batting Average, third in Net Runs, and fifth in Percentage of Games Won.

They finished sixth in Games Ahead of Second and Runs. In addition, the Yanks placed ninth in Net Earned Run Average and tenth in Net Batting Average to round out what is easily the most impressive showing by any of the teams we considered.

Other players made key contributions. Waite Hoyt led the league in wins and ERA. His record was 22—7. Spitballer Urban Shocker was 18—6 and was second in the league in ERA with 2.84. Wilcy Moore, a 29-year old rookie who had perfected a sinker ball, was 19-7. He had a league best 13 saves, which led the league. Herb Pennock was 19—8. The starting pitchers had 82 complete games including 11 shutouts (Yankee pitchers in 1991 had three).

A number of important cogs in this great Yankee machine were provided by the Boston Red Sox, starting with Babe Ruth himself. Cash poor Red Sox owner Harry Frasee dealt The Bambino to the Yankees in 1920. During the next few years, the Yankees acquired from the bean-towners, pitchers Waite Hoyt and Herb Pennock, and third sacker Joe Dugan. Hoyt and Pennock became the aces of the Yankee staff, and both are now enshrined in Cooperstown.

The Bombers won their first six games and held first place every day of the season. One of the highlights of the season was the home run battle between Ruth and Gehrig. Gehrig actually led Ruth 45-44 before being overtaken by the Sultan of Swat.

In the World Series against the Pittsburgh Pirates, the Yankees became the first American League team to win the series in four straight games.

What the Sportswriters Were Writing Then About the Yankees

Here are some excerpts from an article about the 1927 World Series that appeared in the Oct. 12, 1927 *New York Times*:

"The 1927 World Series has passed quickly into baseball history with 10 records smashed and five others tied, chiefly through the batting prowess of Babe Ruth."

And from an article in the Oct. 9 *Times*:

"The Pirates are a better team than they have appeared to be in this series. The strain of a tough campaign has taken its toll. The Buccaneers were stale and tired and never got started.

"And against them was one of the best baseball teams ever gathered together in this broad land, a baseball team which set a new American League record of 110 victories and then climaxed a glorious season by winning four straight World Series games.

"They may not be far wrong who assert that these Yankees are the greatest team in the more than 50 years of baseball history. On his own account, George Herman Ruth demonstrated again that he is the superman of the game. If there was any hero of this series, it was George, with his three singles in the first game, his homer in the second, and his fine hitting yesterday. As Uncle Wilbert Robinson so aptly put it, 'That guy ought to be allowed to play only every other day.'"

And here is how the *Times* described Ruth's last home run in that series:

"Ruth was at the plate now. The count was one and one, when Hill, after wiping the dust off his spectacles, served up a low curve smoking hot. Ruth golfed it and the ball sailed high and far. It climbed uphill while 60,000 shrieked in ecstasy and turned their eyes on the right field bleachers. The brothers Waner turned tail and scooted for the fence. Paul got there first. In fact, he was just in time to look upward and see a badly battered baseball drop limply over the wire screen.

"On the third base coaching line, Arthur Fletcher took his hat off and tossed it high into the air. Some of the fans thought it was a good idea and followed suit. And there was great clamor and tumult and a snowstorm of torn paper. And Carmen Hill looked stunned, like a man who had been suddenly hit on the unprotected chin.

"No, the king is not dead! Long live the king!"

The offensive power of this team can be seen in two of its stars, Babe Ruth and Lou Gehrig. In slugging average, perhaps the most significant of the batting statistics, Ruth holds the record with the highest lifetime average, .690. Gehrig is third at .632.

The spectacular Ruth holds six of the top 10 season records for slugging average, including first, second and third. In 1927, he had the third highest slugging average of all time, at .772. Gehrig had the fourth highest slugging average of all time that same year with .765.

Aditionally, Ruth was second in lifetime home runs with 714 and holds four of the top 10 records for a season, including the second most, 60 in 1927.

In runs batted in, Ruth holds second place for lifetime, with 2,211. Gehrig is third, with 1,990. Gehrig holds three of the top 10 season records, including fourth most for batting in 175 in 1927.

With numbers like these, it is hard to believe he holds the tenth highest lifetime batting average, .342.

Chapter 6
The '39 Yanks and the '29 A's, the Second and Third Best

2. 1939 Yankees

Members of Hall of Fame: 4.

Twelve years after they fielded the greatest team of all time, the Yankees were back with the second best.

But, this time, the "Bronx Bombers" won it with pitching. The 1939 Yankees were the best team of all time in Net Earned Run Average, with a team ERA that was 1.31 points below the league average that year.

The 1939 team was eighth best in Percentage of Games Won, 10th in Games Ahead of Second, tied for first in World Series Net and seventh in Runs Scored.

The Yankee pitchers were led by Red Ruffing who had a record of 21—7. This was his fourth 20-win season in a row. Reliever Johnny Murphy led the league in saves with 19. Lefty Gomez was hampered by a sore arm and had a bad year, for him, with a record of 12-8.

The Yankee attack was led by center fielder Joe DiMaggio. The "Yankee Clipper" led the league in hitting with a .381 average and had 30 home runs. Freshman sensation Charlie Keller in right field batted .334. Red Rolfe at third base batted .329. George Selkirk in left field batted .306 and catcher Bill Dickey, batted .302.

Lou Gehrig, who had played on that great 1927 team, started the year at First but was cut down by his terminal illness early in the season, ending his streak of 2,130 consecutive games played.

Another key to the success of this great team was its fielding. Thus, we find sportswriter John Drebinger writing in the Oct. 2, 1939 *New York Times*:

"The superiority of the McCarthy machine becomes far more pronounced when the fielding exploits are carefully examined. In fact, one of the most extraordinary features of Yankee development in recent years has been a constant trend toward fielding perfection.

"Euphemistically, the Yanks are still styled the 'Bronx Bombers' and their triumphs are most commonly associated with overpowering, crushing attacks. Actually, a strong defense has become more and more the real key to Yankee successes in recent years.

"Never did this shifting of general tactics manifest itself more clearly than during the past season. There were days and long stretches of games this year wherein the Yanks performed with such precision afield as to stamp them as perhaps one of the greatest defensive arrays of all time. . . .

"Granted that when the Yanks needed a batch of runs to win, they invariably had the power to get them. But there were also many days when three runs, two runs, even a single tally sufficed to carry the battle.

"Virtually every manager in the American League this year bemoaned at one time or another the fact that what was really overwhelming them was not the Yankees' vaunted power at the plate but a superb defensive network that kept them throttled at every move. 'How,' as Ossie Vitt expressed it one day, 'can you score against an outfit with an infield you can't squeeze anything through with a shoehorn and an outfield that runs all over the place?' . . .

"So thoroughly has Joe McCarthy worked along defensive lines in his constant tinkering to improve his machine that today we find an American League standard-bearer entering a [World] Series not only holding a defensive advantage but one that must compare favorably with the greatest defensive combinations of all time.

"The foremost defensive improvement this year was, curiously enough, practically forced upon McCarthy when illness ended Lou Gehrig's career. In his place rose a tall, lithe young man who within a few weeks was to stamp himself as one of the finest fielding first sackers of modern times. [Babe] Dahlgren ... has confounded players and critics alike with his amazing stops. . . .

"For the Yanks today, strange as it may sound, are the strongest defensive team in baseball."

In the Oct. 1 *Times*, the same writer commenting on the upcoming World Series wrote that the National League champion Cincinnati Reds would face a "mighty Yankee outfit which for four consecutive campaigns has demolished all opposition in the American League and which now stands poised to close in on its fourth straight world title, a feat without precedence. . . . The American Leaguers, in fact, enter the battle almost prohibitive favorites. They are a 1-to-3 choice to win the series."

A story on the front page of the *Times* of Oct. 9 described the series final game:

"Marse Joe McCarthy's mighty Yankees, beyond question the most amazing club in the 100-year history of baseball, inscribed another brilliant page upon the records of the game today when they crushed the Cincinnati Reds in 10 innings, 7 to 4, to close the 1939 World Series in a whirl of statistics that attested still further to their greatness.

"It gave the American League title holders their fourth straight world championship, an achievement without precedent, as no other team had ever won more than two in a row. . . . Today's victory was also the ninth in a row in series contests."

Then, on Oct. 10, the *Times* wrapped up the four-game series:

"That the job had been done with an amazing thoroughness was a matter that stood out above all else in the series aftermath. Not in any of their previous hollow conquests had the Yanks so dominated a series as they did this one. . . .

"When super pitching was demanded, they had it. When a demonstration of power was in order, they turned that on. . . . The Reds were completely outclassed at every turn. . . . In victory, the outstanding figure was Charlie Keller . . . who gave one of the greatest World Series exhibitions ever turned in by a first year player. . . . In fact, he was the spark that drove the machine to victory in each of the four games."

Some of the players on this team were also on the 1936 Yankee team that was the sixth best of all time; the 1937 Yanks who were 11th best; the 1938 Yanks, the 27th best; the 1941 Yanks, the 26th and the 1942 Yanks, the 25th. And the 1932 Yanks, with players from both the 1927 and 1939 teams, were the tenth best of all.

So, during this 16-year period, the Yankees fielded an unbelievable eight teams out of the 30 best of all time, including the top two and three of the top five. Playing on these eight teams were Hall of Famers Babe Ruth (2 teams), Lou Gehrig (6), Bill Dickey (7 - all but 1927), Joe DiMaggio (6), Tony Lazzeri (4), Earl Combs (2), Lefty Gomez (7 - all but 1927), Waite Hoyt (1), Herb Pennock (2), and Red Ruffing (7 - all but 1927).

And there were other standouts, including Joe Gordon (4), Red Rolfe (7 - all but 1927), Frank Crosetti (7 - all but 1927), Charlie Keller (3), and George Pipgras (2).

In all, the Yankees placed nine teams in the Top 30 (including the 1953 Yanks in a tie for 29th). No other club came close. The Philadelphia Athletics placed four teams in the Top 30 while the New York Giants placed three. Altogether, only 12 different teams finished in the Top 30.

3. 1929 Athletics

Members of Hall of Fame: 4.

Between 1927 and 1932, two of Connie Mack's great Philadelphia Athletics teams challenged the Yankees for the supremacy of baseball.

In fact, the 1929 A's were the third best team of all time. And the 1931 A's were the eighth best.

The '29 A's led the second-place Yankees, still made up of many of the players who had manned the best baseball team in history in 1927, by 18 games and were, as a result, eighth in Games Ahead of Second. They were also tied for tenth in Percentage of Games Won.

Left fielder Al Simmons batted .365 for the A's in 1929 and hit 34 home runs. He also led the league with 157 RBI.

In 1924, Connie Mack began to build another great A's team. He spent over $50,000 for the contract of Al Simmons, and more than $100,000 to sign Robert Moses "Lefty" Grove in 1925. In 1925 the A's also got catcher Mickey Cochrane, who was called by some "a shortstop in shin pads," for $50,000.

In 1926, Mack signed Jimmie Foxx at the age of 17. A First baseman, "Double X" batted .354 in 1929, while hitting 33 homers and batting in 117 runs.

Simmons, Grove, Cochrane and Foxx all became members of the Hall of Fame.

Speedy Mule Haas in center field hit .313. Cochrane was superb behind the plate and batted .331. Lefty Grove, who won 20 and lost 6, led the league in ERA with a 2.81. Six foot, four inch George Earnshaw led the league in wins with a record of 24—8.

As the 1929 World Series approached, the A's 66-year-old manager, Connie Mack, was already a legend. As reported in the *New York Times* on Oct. 4, 1929, "For Connie Mack, this coming fall classic will be nothing new. He's already been in five of them dating across a stretch of 24 years. . . . Mack's experience. . . should count. Mack is the accepted master tactician of the diamond. The adroitness with which he arranges his battle array is almost uncanny."

"With the enduring patience of a hermit of the desert, he waited and persevered 15 years for this moment. . . . Mack, an outstanding figure in the American League since its inception, piloted his first Athletic team to victory in 1902. By 1914, he had added five more pennants and three world's titles to his record. Then he dismantled a great team regarded by many as the greatest team of all time, and after a lapse of 15 years, he is back with another grand array."

In the same article, Ty Cobb was quoted calling Mack the greatest manager ever.

The 1929 World Series against the Chicago Cubs turned out to be one of the most exciting ever, despite the fact the Athletics won four of five games. (The one won by the Cubs was the first World Series game taken by a National League team in three years as the Yankees had swept the 1927 and 1928 series.)

The first two games of the World Series were played before 51,000 fans in Wrigley Field in Chicago. The

Times reported Oct. 9 that "a man of 35 . . . stole all the thunder of the opening game of the World Series of 1929 today. . . . His name is Howard Ehmke, chosen to pitch only 15 minutes before game time by the crafty Connie Mack. He went on to hurl the Athletics to victory over the Cubs by a score of 3 to 1, setting a new World Series strike-out record of 13."

The Cubs had expected George Earnshaw, "right-handed ace of the Mack forces to pitch, and if not him, then one of the left-handed fireballers, Bob Grove or Rube Wahlberg."

The A's also won the second game, in Chicago. But then the Cubs won the third, in Philadelphia, by a 3-1 score, setting up the fourth game, one of the most unusual in World Series history.

As reported in the *Times* of Oct. 13, "It happened in the seventh inning . . . at a time when more than 30,000 spectators sat in the packed stands at Shibe Park steeped in despair. . . . The Athletics, beaten the third game yesterday, were trailing 8-0. . . . Then the surging Mack attack flattened all before it to roll up a total of 10 runs for the inning. And so, to the Athletics, went the fourth game of the series by a score of 10-8."

"Never in all World Series history was there such an inning. Records large and small collapsed in wholesale lots. . . . For six innings, Charlie Root . . . appeared on his way to a merited revenge [for his first game loss]. . . . He had held the mightiest of Mack sluggers in a grip of iron, allowing only three scattered hits. And while Charlie was doing this, the Cubs . . . cuffed and battered four of Connie Mack's prize hurlers. They hammered Jack Quinn. . . . They pulverized Rube Wahlberg and smashed Ed Rommel."

In the big inning, which surpassed by two the World Series record for most runs in one inning, Al Simmons,

Mule Haas and Jimmy Dykes all had two hits. One of Simmons' was a lead off home run. The A's were helped by an inside-the-park home run that Hack Wilson, Cub center fielder, lost in the sun. But the hit that won the game was a low hard liner by Dykes to left that brought home the final two runs.

"Riggs Stephenson," the *Times* reported, "chased it desperately and got both hands on the ball but failed to hold it. It bounded away for a two-base hit."

Yet, even after this heart-breaking loss, the Cubs did not give up. Playing before President Herbert Hoover and 31,000 other fans in Shibe Park, the Cubs took a 2-0 lead into the last half of the ninth.

The Oct. 15 *Times* described what happened next, "There has never been a World Series quite like this one and certainly no such ending as that of this afternoon when the Athletics with one dynamic thrust in the last half of the ninth rolled back a fighting team of Cubs to win the fifth game of the series. The score was 3 to 2."

For eight innings, Cub pitcher Pat Malone had limited the A's to two hits. In the ninth, Mule Haas homered with a man on to tie the score. Al Simmons doubled. Bing Miller doubled to score Simmons with the winning run.

"For the second successive game," the *Times* report continued, "the Athletics had come from nowhere to snatch a victory from defeat. And this time the triumph was final. Men and women screeched until they were purple. . . . President Hoover understood and smiled for he had been an eyewitness to one of the most amazing spectacles an American sporting event could provide."

Mack had become the first manager to win four World Series.

Chapter 7
Fourth, Fifth and Sixth: Cubs, Pirates and Yanks

4. 1906 Cubs

Members of Hall of Fame: 4.

The 1906 Chicago Cubs hold the records for most games won in a season, 116, and for the highest Percentage of Games Won, .763. They were third in Games Ahead of Second. In addition, they were second in Earned Run Average among all pennant winners.

This team starred the famous double play combination of Tinker to Evers to Chance. Playing Manager and first baseman Frank Chance batted .319. Third baseman Harry Steinfeldt batted .327 with a league-leading 83 RBI. The catcher, Johnny Kling, batted .312.

Kling was an outstanding catcher, later named by Hall of Famer Honus Wagner as "the all-time greatest catcher."

Mordechi "Three Finger" Brown, who lost most of the index finger on his pitching hand in a childhood accident, led the league in earned run average with 1.04, still a National League record. He also led the league in wins with a record of 26—6. Ten of his wins were shutouts. Jack Pfiester was 20—8. Their pitchers had a total of 28 shutouts including nine 1-0 wins.

Chance came to the Cubs as a catcher and was converted to first base. He became outstanding at that position. He was promoted to manager in 1905.

Joe Tinker started out at third base but was converted to shortstop. He became a Hall of Famer, as did his partner, 115-pound second baseman, Johnny Evers.

Down the Stretch, during the month of August, the Cubs won 26 and lost only 3.

The 1907 Cubs, made up of almost the same players, were the 17th best team of all time. They also won National League pennants in 1908 and 1910.

On Oct. 7, 1906, a review of the season just completed appeared in the *New York Times*:

"The feature of the year has undoubtedly been the performance of the Chicago National League club which will succeed the Giants as champions. Finishing third in the race of last year, the western team from the start of the present campaign showed itself, along with Pittsburgh, to be the most dangerous rival of the world's champions, and since its success has rated as the best organized team ever seen on the field.

"With a record of victories unprecedented in the history of the sport, it has taken the series from every other club in the league by a good margin, and since July 1st last, has continued to lead uninterruptedly. New York's last desperate attempt to dislodge the Chicagos was in the Polo Grounds in August when Manager McGraw by piratical tactics threw away a game by refusing Umpire Johnstone admission to the grounds and losing two of the other three. This series was undoubtedly the Waterloo of the present champions."

However, the Cubs would lose the World Series to their crosstown rivals, the White Sox, in a stunning six game upset. The *Times* summed up the final game and Series outcome on Oct. 15:

"CHICAGO. OCT. 14. The Chicago club of the American League is the champion of the world. By winning today's game 8-3 against the Chicago club of the National League, the Americans earned the right to float the world's championship pennant as well as the pennant of the American League.

"Today's game was the sixth of the series and the fourth victory for the Americans. The attendance was 19,249. . . .

"When the last National batsman had gone out and the fact that new champions had been freshly created burned its impress on thousands of excited minds, a crowd surged around the box wherein sat Charles W. Murphy, president of the losing club. He smiled gamely at requests for a speech and said, 'The best team won. They won because they played the better ball. Too much praise cannot be given to President Comiskey and Captain Jones and the team which by unprecedented pluck climbed in midseason from seventh place to the top of their own league and then topped off that great accomplishment by winning the world's championship from the team that made a runaway race of the National League contest. I call for three cheers for Comiskey and his great team.'

"Among the expert critics of baseball it is generally admitted that to the American pitchers most of the credit is due. . . . The American pitchers were effective when hits meant runs, particularly against such men as Chance, Schulte, Steinfeldt and Kling."

5. 1902 Pirates

Members of Hall of Fame: 3.

The 1902 Pittsburgh Pirates were second in Percentage of Games Won and were first in Games Ahead of Second, with 27 1/2. They were also first in both Net Batting Average and Net Runs. They were sixth in Net Slugging Average.

Ginger Beaumont, the Pirate center fielder, led the league in hitting with a batting average of .357. The third baseman, Tommy Leach, led the league in home runs with six! "The Dutchman" Honus Wagner, who played outfield, shortstop and first base, batted .329 and had a league-leading 91 RBI. Jack Chesbro led the league in wins with a record of 28 and 6.

"At an early stage [of the season]," the *New York Times* reported Oct. 5, 1902, "the victory of Pittsburgh's players was a foregone conclusion. It was generally conceded that the playing strength of the champions was too great a handicap to overcome by the other contesting teams. This had an injurious effect on the gate receipts of the other contesting teams."

The World Series did not start until 1903.

6. 1936 Yankees

Members of Hall of Fame: 6.

This was the first Yankee team to win a pennant without Babe Ruth. He had been released by the Yankees following the 1934 season.

The 1936 Yankees were first in Runs Scored with 1,065. They were second in Net Home Runs and fourth in Net Slugging Average. They were fifth in Games Ahead of Second, seventh in Net Runs Scored and ninth in Batting Average.

Lou Gehrig led the league in homers with 49 and batted .354. Bill Dickey batted .362, still the highest average ever for a catcher.

This was also Joe DiMaggio's first year with the Yanks. He played left field and batted .323 with 29 home runs and 125 RBI.

A number of recent newcomers also contributed heavily to the Yankee excellence. They included George Selkirk and Jake Pail in the outfield, Red Rolfe at third base, and Monte Parson and Bump Hadley, pitching. Powell in center field batted .306. Rolfe hit .319. Selkirk in right hit .308.

Red Ruffing won 20 and lost 12.

A *New York Times* article on Sept. 23, 1936, reported that in beating the Athletics 10-3 the Yanks became the first team in history with five players who had batted in 100 or more runs in one season. In the game, George Selkirk batted in his 100th run, joining Lou Gehrig, Bill Dickey, Joe DiMaggio and Tony Lazzeri, at this RBI plateau.

In a three-part series starting Sept. 26, John Drebinger of the *Times* compared the Yanks and their World Series foe, the New York Giants:

"Although the tendency in the two major leagues over a long stretch has been to develop upon strikingly contrasting lines, the American League stressing offense and the National circuit pinning its hopes on defense, perhaps no series in recent years has seen this difference so pronounced as promises to be the case in the forthcoming clash between the Yankees and Giants. . . .

"The Yankees hammered their entire circuit into submission with an attack which surpassed even the dazzling records of the slugging Yankee teams during the Ruthian era or the gorgeous Mack creations of six or seven years ago. . . . As for the Yanks, their pitching was commendable enough, but only so far as exigencies demanded. . . . Of the entire Yankee cast, only one hurler really lives with the chance of spinning a game which might match the [Carl] Hubbell performance. He is Lefty Gomez. . . .

"[The Yankees'] confidence lies in the firm belief that they can hammer back any runs that might slip away from them. . . .

"For when a club sets up a record of fence-smashing

achievement as have the Yankees this year, the . . . question at once becomes, how much of this is due to really great hitting, how much to weak pitching?

"It must be conceded that the McCarthy forces will bring into this series a far superior offensive. In their own circuit this year, the feats of the Yanks were truly amazing. . . . They set a new all-time record for hitting home runs. Even more remarkable was their feat of having five regulars in the lineup each of whom drove in more than 100 runs. In the entire National League, there were only six players who topped the 100 mark. . . .

"After the passing of their first great "Murderers' Row" under the Huggins regime, it used to be said of the Yanks that if a pitcher got by Ruth and Gehrig, 90% of his troubles were over. But, even with the Babe out and only Lou carrying on, a pitcher's troubles with the present day Yanks never seem to cease. And when Charlie Ruffing, the best-hitting pitcher in baseball, is in the lineup, the Yanks can muster a solid front of nine high-grade hitters. Gehrig . . . tops the field, the most powerful clouter in baseball today.

"DiMaggio, the phenomenal freshman, has also definitely established himself as an extremely dangerous and hard clouter. . . . But, perhaps the smartest of the lot is Dickey and this on the say so of no less an authority on the subject than Hubbell, himself. . . . And when you add to these a secondary array including Selkirk, Crosetti, and the ever dangerous Lazzeri, as well as Powell and Rolfe, one can easily understand what a pitcher has to worry about when he stacks up against the Yanks. . . .

"In addition to their normal hitting power, the Yankee attack is further enhanced by superior speed.

"Joe McCarthy today stands out as one of the greatest team-builders of modern times. . . . [He has had] a most amazing record over a period of 11 campaigns divided almost equally in the two leagues. . . . [In 1926], Marse Joe . . . took the last-place Cubs, and with a few deft touches, bounced the team into the first division. . . . From then on the Cubs, long in the doldrums, once again became a vital factor in National League flag races. They won the pennant in 1929 and just missed in 1930. . . .

"In 1931, he came to the Yanks. It was a critical moment in the fortunes of that club, for a one-time great machine was cracking up. . . . McCarthy, with a few master strokes, moved it up, moving it from third to second and from there to a pennant in 1932. . . . This year, he proved much too strong for the good of the entire league. . . . As with the Cubs, he rebuilt the Yanks . . . with rare shrewdness. He is an amazing judge of ballplayers, young and old. Even the team that won the 1932 pennant has been more than half recast. The Rolfes, Selkirks, DiMaggios and Powells are no accidents. . . .

"As a field leader, however, McCarthy can not rate with the truly great strategists of the diamond. . . . There is a certain hesitancy to some of his field directing that at times becomes strongly noticeable. . . . McCarthy's forte seems to lie in building great ball clubs and then letting them roll. If they prove strong enough, they will win. If not, they will finish a strong second or third."

On Oct. 3, with the series underway, the *Times* reported:

"The Yankees spattered a dozen marks in the log of World Series history yesterday as they drove Bill Terry and his Giants to the verge of distraction."

The story pointed out that the Yanks set 12 new World Series records in their 18-4 game 2 win, including most runs in a game (18), largest margin of victory (14), and the first time all nine men hit safely and scored.

"For driving a man to distraction," the story continued, "the Yanks must have at least equalled anything ever before done to Terry." The Yanks won the series four games to two.

Chapter 8
Seventh to Tenth: Cards Twice, A's and Yanks

7. 1944 Cardinals

Members of Hall of Fame: 1.

The 1944 St. Louis Cardinals were seventh in Net Earned Run Average.

The Cards were led by outfielder Stan Musial who batted .347. Third baseman Whitey Kurowski led the team in homers with 20. Johnny Hopp in center batted .336. Walker Cooper, the catcher, hit .317. Mort Cooper, his pitcher brother, won 22 and lost 7. Max Lanier was 17 and 12. Rookie Ted Wilks was 17-4.

The Cards were an outstanding team. Almost the same personnel made up the 1943 Cards, the 10th best team, and the 1942 Cards, the 19th best.

Writer John Drebinger looked ahead to the upcoming World Series versus the St. Louis Browns, matching two St. Louis teams for the only time in baseball history in an article appearing in the Oct. 3, 1944 *New York Times*:

"[The Cards] started the season with a team that had lost practically nothing of the strength which made it a decisive pennant winner the previous season whereas virtually all others in both loops had lost heavily to the military draft. . . . The result was inevitable. They spreadeagled their field so swiftly there was no sem-

blance of competition in their circuit by midseason. . . .
And then suddenly, almost overnight, something passed
out of Billy Southworth's invincibles. They began to
lose. . . .

"They continued to flounder throughout September
and it is because they stumbled right up until the last
that the experts today are scratching their heads as they
wonder whether Southworth can yet succeed in rekin-
dling the winning spark. Even now, by any standard of
measurement . . . the Cards stand head and shoulders
above their rivals. They have a powerful,
well-distributed attack. . . . They have a fine infield
woven around the matchless Marty Marion, they are
capable of throwing up an almost flawless defense and
their hurling staff, headed by Mort Cooper, Harry
Brecheen, Ted Wilks and Max Lanier, is well-balanced
and effective.

Arthur Daley of the *Times* described the Cardinals'
series victory Oct. 9:

"The bubble burst today for the Brownies. . . . The
Redbirds today were the masterful aristocrats they were
all season. They hit well, fielded well and received excellent pitching. . . .

"The Cards gathered themselves together to square
the series at two all and then they took complete control of the next two frays. . . . The series ended as it
should have ended, in a Cardinal triumph."

Were the Wartime Card Teams Really Any Good?
Do these wartime Card teams rank this high simply because competition was weak with so many of the great
stars of the game in uniform or are they just the strongest of a weak lot?

A lot of major leaguers were in the service by 1944,
fewer in 1943 and fewer still in 1942. (The U.S. did not

get into the war until after the Pearl Harbor attack, Dec. 7, 1941.)

For example, here is the situation with the Brooklyn Dodgers, who won the National League pennant in 1941. Only one of their eight starting position players, third baseman Cookie Lavagetto, missed the 1942 season nor did any of their four principal starting pitchers. However, two additional position players missed 1943 and two more missed 1944, leaving the Dodgers with only three of the eight starting position players from the pennant winning squad.

In addition, they still had three of their four starting pitchers in 1943 and two of the four in 1944. Thus, 1942 was little affected by the war, with the effect increasing in 1943 and then, again, in 1944.

One can argue that if virtually the same Cardinal team was the 19th best of all time in 1942, when baseball was only marginally impacted by the war, and 10th best in 1943, with more effect, then it is not unreasonable to state that the 1944 team was also an outstanding one in any era. Perhaps not seventh best, but still quite good. Hall of Famer Stan Musial played on all three teams and *he* is a Hall of Famer in any era.

Based upon the excerpts earlier from the *New York Times*, it could be argued that the 1944 team could have had a better statistical record if their competition had been better. The Cardinals were blowing away the field in August before apparently losing interest in September.

We also looked at how the statistical performance of players in 1944 compared with 1941 and 1942 and with 1946 and 1947. Of six position players on the 1944 team whose names we recognized, only two had their highest batting average in 1944 - Johnny Hopp and Walker Cooper - although four of the six had batting averages in 1944 higher than their lifetime averages. Three of the four 1944 pitchers had lower ERAs in 1944 than in the other four years.

We also looked at players whose names we recognized on the second, third and fourth place teams in 1944 (Pirates, Reds and Cubs). We came up with eight players. Only one had a higher batting average in 1944 than in the two prewar or two postwar years. However, four of the eight batted higher in 1944 than they did lifetime.

We looked at six National League pitchers from these three teams. Only three had lower ERAs in 1944 than in the other four years. However, five had lower ERAs in 1944 than lifetime.

In the American League, we also looked at players on the top four teams (Browns, Tigers, Yankees, and Red Sox) whose names we recognized. We came up with 10 players. Six hit higher in 1944 than in the two prewar or two postwar years and eight were higher in 1944 than lifetime.

We looked at nine American League pitchers. Six had lower ERAs in 1944 than in the other four years. All nine had lower ERAs than lifetime.

Weak pitching did not increase home run output. Only two of the six Cardinals hit more home runs in 1944 than in one of the other four years. Only two of the eight players from other National League teams and only two of the 10 American League players did so.

All of this indicates to us that the caliber of baseball played in 1944, while not at the same level as before or after the war, was not very far below.

8. 1931 Athletics

Members of Hall of Fame: 4.

The 1931 Philadelphia Athletics were sixth among all pennant winners in Percentage of Games Won and tenth in Net Earned Run Average.

Al Simmons in left field led the league in batting with a .390 average. First baseman Jimmie Foxx had 30 home runs and 120 runs batted in. Mule Haas in center batted .323. Mickey Cochrane, the catcher, batted .349. Lefty Grove led the league in wins and ERA. He was 31 and 4. Rube Walberg was 20 and 12. George Earnshaw was 21 and 7.

John Drebinger began analyzing the approaching World Series between these Athletics and the St. Louis Cardinals in the Sept. 28, 1931 *New York Times.* First, he looked at their defenses:

"Of necessity, then, it becomes quite clear that all pennant winning teams must possess excellent defensive qualities to mesh with the attack and such we find to be the case with the Athletics and Cardinals. . . . Each slightly excels the other in the two departments of defensive play.

"The Mackmen hold the edge in pitching . . . and the Cardinals have a shade in fielding. . . .

"And as the World Series at best is nothing more than a short swift moving sprint, Connie Mack, holding a pair of mighty right and left bowers, must be conceded the better hand. [Lefty] Grove's amazing work during the past year in which he has won 31 games and lost only 4 easily stamps the tall southpaw as one of the game's greatest hurlers, if not the greatest of all time, either left handed or right handed. And directly behind him comes the towering [George] Earnshaw who did such heroic work last fall and seems fully capable of repeating the performance this year.

"Unless something should go amiss at the last minute, these two are certain to carry the brunt of the work again for Mack as they did last year with Mahaffey and [Waite] Hoyt, who suddenly seems to have effected a singular rejuvenation."

Drebinger added that in the field, "Only behind the plate is there a decided Mack advantage, for Cochrane is still Cochrane and the game's greatest catcher."

"Summed up, then, the Mackmen control the pitching; the Cards, the fielding and as pitching obviously rates higher than fielding, the final defensive advantage must be conceded to the Athletics."

The next day, Drebinger looked at the offenses:

"It is, of course, offensive power that wins games and pennants. Both the Athletics and Cardinals carry an abundance of attacking force. . . .

"The Mackmen finished absolutely last in base stealing in their league this last year. . . . The power of their attack lies in their bats. That is a tremendous power, far more forceful than that possessed by the Cardinals. . . .

"The bulk of the Mack attacking force is concentrated in a small group that acts with dynamic effect. In this group are to be found Simmons, Cochrane, Haas, and Foxx, with Miller also lending a helping hand. When a couple of men get on base just before this array comes to bat, the Mackmen at once are poised for sweeping attack for all are sure-fire hitters. . . .

"It is for this reason therefore that the edge in attack must be conceded to the Athletics. . . .

"Before concluding, a word here might not be amiss on the ball which for the first time offers a difference between the two leagues.

"That the less lively ball in vogue in the National

League this year has made a marked difference in the batting of certain hitters cannot be denied. . . . But what effect the less lively ball will have on the Mackmen in the games played in the National League park or how the livelier American League ball will influence the Cardinals while playing in Philadelphia cannot even be guessed."

The Athletics had been established as 2 to 1 favorites in the series, according to the Sept. 29 *Times*.

However, the Cardinals captured the World Series in seven games. On Oct. 12, the *Times* reported on the surprising outcome:

"Twelve record performances marked the 1931 World Series. . . . The Cardinals, led by Pepper Martin, came close to running wild through the record books. They won the series, but Martin's personal rampage was effectively stopped by Grove and Earnshaw in the last two games."

Despite the Cardinals' series upset, Grove won two games for the A's against one loss. Earnshaw won one and lost two. Waite Hoyt, the old Yankee star, lost the other for the A's. Earnshaw's only win was the only shutout in the series.

9. 1943 Cardinals

Members of Hall of Fame: 1.

In his second major league season, Stan Musial led the league in batting with .357. Walker Cooper, the catcher, batted .318. Mort Cooper led the league in wins. His record was 21 and 8.

Arthur Daley of the *New York Times* looked ahead to the upcoming World Series against the Yankees in this Oct. 5, 1943 report:

"A year ago at this time the Yankees were a shocked and disillusioned ball club. The Cardinals, in case you have forgotten, had just beaten them in the World Series. . . . Yankee pride took a worse drubbing last year than the Yankee team. . . .

"The label on the Cardinal package still reads 'Handle With Care.' It will be with only delicacy and respect that the home forces attempt to unwrap it. . . .

"The fast moving operatives of Billy Southworth's ball club are a mighty slick ball club. They have the game's leading hitter in Stan Musial and the game's best catcher in Walker Cooper. They have good balance.

"But, in one important respect they differ from one year ago. Billy the Kid does not have the rock-bound pitching staff he had then. . . . Mort Cooper supposedly has bobbed up with a sore arm. Ernie White definitely has one. . . .

On Oct. 2, John Drebinger of the *Times* gave his views on what to expect in the series:

"The two contenders are remarkably well matched on the surface. Defensively, the Cards look to have the edge. But, that vanishes quickly when one includes in the calculation that most valuable of all defensive factors - pitching.

"Similarly, on the attack, the Cards have averaged consistently higher than the Yanks all year. . . . Yet, in the all important matter of driving in runs and clouting homers, the Yanks excel.

"Most experienced baseball men rate hurling 70% of the game with the percentage even higher in World Series play. . . . The Cards . . . enter with only one ace and he suffers the psychological disadvantage of having been trumped several times by the rival league. Mort Cooper for two years has been the National's top player, but was floored twice by the Yanks last fall. . . .

"Behind Cooper, the Cards must bank on Max Lanier and the youngsters, Alpha Brazle, Harry Brecheen and

George Munger with the chief assets of the first three lying in the fact that they are left handed. The Yanks on occasion have experienced trouble with lefties. . . .

"At other points, however, the Cards show to advantage. Bill Dickey and Walker Cooper are a standoff behind the plate, but the Cards' infield, actually better than last year, has the edge while in the outfield the St. Louis superiority is even more pronounced despite the losses of Terry Moore and Enos Slaughter.

"Charlie Keller may stand off Johnny Hopp in left but Harry Walker and Stan Musial defensively are well ahead of any combination the Yanks have to offer in center and right among Johnny Lindell, Bud Matheny, Tuck Stainback and Roy Weatherly.

The next day, Drebinger commented on how this series was overshadowed by World War II:

"One of the few institutions to survive so far the ravages of an all-out global war, baseball's World Series once again moves into the spotlight. . . . Millions . . . will listen in throughout the nation, even from the outermost posts of America's far-flung battle lines.

"Only one slight alteration has been found necessary to meet the wartime needs. . . . Instead of only the first two games being staged in the opening city, the first three will be held here. . . . That will be the last New York will see of the series regardless of the outcome as all the remaining games will be played in St. Louis. . . .

"As was the case a year ago, war charities will benefit [by receiving] a share of the receipts."

The Yankees somewhat unexpectedly took the series in five games.

Arthur Daley reported on how it happened in the Oct. 12 *Times*:

"The Yankees . . . captured the final game of the series . . . in the old Yankee way, an explosive home run off the bat of the soft-spoken 'Arkansas Traveller,' Bill Dickey.

"The Cards had their chances today, but they were utterly unable to take any advantage of them. . . . The operation was performed in nearly as painless a fashion as possible, four out of five games.

"The Yanks outran the wild-running Cards. They outpitched them. And they came through when they had to like the champions they are."

Among the Cardinal pitchers ineligible for series duty who nevertheless arrived to pitch batting practice were Lieutenant Johnny Beazley, Sergeant Enos Slaughter, Private Jimmy Brown and Private Terry Moore. The final Cardinal pitcher during the fifth game was Murry Dickson who had already been inducted into the Army and was on furlough.

10. 1932 Yankees

Members of Hall of Fame: 9.

The Yankees were back as American League champions after a three year absence. They beat the 1931 champion Athletics by 13 games.

The 1932 Yankees were third in Runs Scored and fifth in Net Runs. They were eighth in Net Home Runs and ninth in both Percentage of Games Won and Net Slugging Average. They tied for first in World Series Net.

Babe Ruth batted .341 and hit 41 homers for this team. He had 137 RBI. First baseman Lou Gehrig batted .349 with 34 home runs and 151 runs batted in. Earle Combs, the center fielder, hit .321. Bill Dickey, the catcher, batted .310.

Three pitchers stood out. Lefty Gomez was 24—7. Red Ruffing was 18—7. Johnny Allen was 17—4.

John Drebinger of the *New York Times* presented a three-part preview of the World Series to be played against the Cubs. On Sept. 24, 1932, he wrote:

"It being generally accepted by the outstanding savants of the game that baseball, like all Gaul, is divided into three parts, the defense, offense, and general strategy. It seems logical enough to assume this basis to be as practical as any for comparing the relative merits of the Yankees and the Cubs. . . .

"True, many teams have won pennants by being extremely well fortified in one, but few, if any, have triumphed without combining a liberal share of all three.

"Taking up the defense first. . . . The Cubs hold the strongest unit, with a lot of quick outside tricks to boot. . . .

"Against all this, the Yankees have a staff which, while a good one, nevertheless has about it a certain air of uncertainty. The brilliant left hander, Gomez, has done some sensational work this year but he did a large part of it during the fore part of the campaign.

"Recently he has been prone to show himself considerably less effective. Tall and slender, he is not a robust fellow and the strain of the early months may have sapped more of his strength than he can recover.

"Pipgras, too, has been inclined to be a bit uncertain, thus leaving Ruffing as the one sure-fire ace. "Big Red," in fact, looks like the Yanks' best bet and physically and mentally he is well equipped to play the part. Johnny Allen, though young and inexperienced, also promises to be a strong card. . . .

"The Yanks also have in the background a grand campaigner of other years, the talented left-hander, Herbie Pennock who, if the fighting gets close and in any way desperate, is almost certain to be called upon for assistance.

"Better balance and swifter movement seem to give the Cubs the edge in the infield where the Yankees have had a serious flaw at shortstop which has not yet been satisfactorily ironed out."

The article pointed out that old Yankee shortstop, Mark Koenig, now performing for the Cubs, gave the Cubs "a decided advantage over either of the Yankee shortstops, Crosetti or Lary." The author said that Billy Herman of the Cubs was a better second baseman than Tony Lazzeri.

Drebinger continued, "Gehrig in recent years has developed into a fine, dependable first baseman, but he is not quite the accomplished performer we find in Grimm and while Sewell, at third, has been a big factor in the Yankee success this year by his remarkable steadiness, he is not quite as nimble a ground coverer as Woody English.

"Behind the plate . . . it is practically a standoff between Hartnett and Dickey.

"In the outfield, Cuyler, Stephenson and Moore also give the Cubs a fielding edge for though both Combs and Chapman are very capable performers, Ruth can no longer cover the ground with any of the Chicagoans. Especially will he be at a disadvantage in Chicago where left field, which he will have to play to avoid the sun in right, takes in a much wider territory than the Babe's favorite right field pasture at the stadium."

In the Sept. 26 issue of the *Times*, Drebinger compared the two teams on offense:

"[During the season,] the Yanks unfolded a high-powered, dynamic attack that completely overshadowed anything the Cubs had to offer. . . .

"Ruth and Gehrig are the ace cannonadeers. . . . And directly behind this pair come such able clouters as Combs, Lazzeri, Dickey, and Chapman with Sewell also closing out a season in which he has done some unusually effective swatting.

"It is a formidable array and so well spread out as to give a rival pitcher scarcely a breathing spell. If the upper half of the batting order is momentarily checked, the lower half is apt to break out at any moment."

Drebinger concluded the next day that in "the department of strategic manoeuvers," Yankee Manager Joe McCarthy, "must be conceded a strong advantage" over Chicago's Manager Charley Grimm who held "a meager hand."

On Sept. 22, *Times* columnist John Kieran who later became one of the stars of the radio program, "Information Please," wrote:

"G. Herman Ruth is warming up for his tenth World Series. . . . For seven or eight years in a Yankee uniform the Babe was a fine outfielder and one of the best throwers in the major leagues. Nobody paid much attention to these minor items. His home run clouting overshadowed these little things.

"It is almost forgotten now that this same Babe Ruth was one of the great left-handed pitchers of his day on the mound. . . .

Kieran noted that Ruth pitched the opening game of the 1918 World Series for the Boston Red Sox against the Cubs and added:

"He shut them out, 1-0. That made 22 consecutive scoreless innings for him as a World Series pitcher. He came back again in the fourth game to shut them out for seven innings, making a total of 29 scoreless innings for him. He won the game, 3-2. . . .

"The Babe came to the Yankees in 1920 and in 1921, the Yankees won their first pennant. . . . The Yanks have won six pennants since that time. . . .

"There remains the overwhelming fact that Babe

Ruth is going into his 10th World Series and seventh as the heavy hitting outfielder of the Yankees. Teams rise and fall. Players come and go, but the Babe has managed to work his way into a record number of World Series. There must have been some connection between the presence of G. Herman Ruth on a team and the presence of that team in a World Series."

On Oct. 3, the *Times* wrapped up the Yankees' series sweep:

"The 1932 World Series was featured by 17 outstanding additions to the list of championship records. Altogether, in four games, 15 records were broken and two others were equalled. Babe Ruth featured in exactly 13 record feats."

Ruth's **new** records included most home runs in all World Series (15); most total bases in all series (96); most long hits, all series (22); most walks, all series (33); most strike-outs, all series (30); most series (10); most runs, all series (37); most runs batted in, all series (33); most runs batted in, one game (4); most times played on world championship club (7); most times batted .300 or more in a series (6).

And on the *Times* front page the same day, John Drebinger reported:

"The mighty New York Yankees smashed their way to another decisive victory over the Chicago Cubs today and captured the 1932 World Series in four straight games. . . .

"The score was 13 to 6, which in very cold figures should leave little to the imagination as to how thoroughly the team managed by Joseph E. McCarthy outclassed its rivals. It marked the third time that the Yankees, with Babe Ruth and Lou Gehrig in the cast, have recorded a clean World Series sweep. . . .

"[It] gave to this amazing ball club the added record,

unparalleled in baseball, of having won 12 consecutive World Series games. . . . Never were the Ruppert [the Yankee owner] forces more devastating than they were this afternoon."

Times sports columnist John Kieran reviewed the series in similar fashion Oct. 4:

"At times it looked as though Lou Gehrig could wallop them single-handed. . . .

"Through the run of the major league season, there were many critics who called the Chicago pitching staff the best in either league. . . . The Cubs made 19 runs in four games and didn't win a single contest. The old Cubs in 1907 scored the same number of runs against the Detroit Tigers and didn't lose a game. . . . If that last game had gone another inning or so, Manager Charley Grimm would have had to summon [Cub officials] Bill Veeck or P. K. Wrigley to the mound. . . .

"An odd point about this series was that the Yankees rolled happily through four straight victories without being even close to their best form. . . . There were times in this series when the onlookers must have thought that pitchers of the old type were extinct with the dodo and the passenger pigeon. . . .

"In some quarters this is being heralded as the best of Yankee ball clubs or at least the equal of any that preceded it. The vote in this corner still goes to the Yankees of 1927. . . .

"That was the club Uncle Wilbert called the superior of the Old Orioles, thus bringing down on his head the wrath of the elders for whom the Old Orioles will always be the one perfect team in baseball annals."

Chapter 9
11th thru 14th: Yanks, Orioles, A's and Giants

11. 1937 Yankees

Members of Hall of Fame: 6.

This Yankee squad finished fifth in both Runs and Net Earned Run Average among the pennant winners. They were also sixth in Net Home Runs.

Joe DiMaggio, in his second season, moved to center field and led the league in home runs with 46 while batting .346 and 167 RBI. First baseman Lou Gehrig batted .351 with 37 home runs and 159 RBI. Bill Dickey batted .332 with 29 homers and 133 runs batted in.

Lefty Gomez led the league in pitching with 21 wins against 11 losses. He also topped the A.L. with an ERA of 2.33. Red Ruffing was 20—7.

For the second consecutive year, the Yanks met their crosstown foes, the Giants, in the World Series. In the sports pages of the Oct. 2, 1937 *New York Times*, John Drebinger compared the defenses of the two teams:

"[This year], the Yankees are brilliantly equipped with two brilliant flingers, capable on one of their good days of winning a World Series behind any pennant winner . . . Ruffing and Gomez.

"Ruffing . . . has had a remarkable year. He is steady, strong and smart, with a splendid assortment of so-called stuff. And as for Gomez, to say our singular southpaw is 100 per cent a better pitcher than a year ago is putting it conservatively. . . .

"In the outfield, DiMaggio is a star of the first magnitude and quite overshadows Wally Berger. . . . [However], the edge on defense remains with the National Leaguers."

On Oct. 4, Drebinger looked at the offenses:

"As the Yanks moved on the World Series last fall, they constituted beyond question the most devastating ball club ever assembled surpassing even the achievements of the same club during the Ruthian era in the last decade. . . . There simply was no rest for a pitcher facing those Yanks of 1936. . . .

"Of the five who drove in more than 100 runs in 1936, only three - DiMaggio, Gehrig and Dickey - moved into that select circle this year . . . so, while the Yanks still hold the advantage on the offense by virtue of their superior record, their margin . . . is far less than it was 12 months ago."

John Kieran gave his view in the *Times* the next day:

"The Yankees in recent weeks were merely sauntering to a pennant. The Giants took theirs on the dead run. They had to sprint to make it. . . .

"Yankee rooters have been raving about Lefty Gomez and Cholly the Red Ruffing. . . . But on the last day of the season Manager McCarthy sent Monty Pearson against the rich Red Sox and Monty gave what might be called a display. He had everything. . . .

"In advance, the pitching seems to be a standoff. . . . Messrs. DiMaggio, Gehrig and Dickey . . . have hammered out almost as many home runs as all the Giants put together. . . . The big problem of the Giant pitchers will be to get [these] three men out.. . . "The odd thing about those Yankees is that any one of them may slam out a long hit at any time. . . .

"One thing about this series is that no one will steal it. . . . Base running is a lost art as far as these contenders are concerned. . . . Frank Crosetti tops both rosters with 12."

The Yankees won the World Series four games to one. John Kieran summed up their near sweep this way:

"Marse Joe McCarthy's men overpowered [the Giants] in all directions. The Yanks had the pitching and the hitting and even in the field, where the Giants were supposed to present an airtight defense, the American Leaguers had it all over their National League opponents.

"From the very start, the Yankees acted as if they considered it their series. The way they ran the bases was enough to indicate that. . . . The Giants were hesitant, even timorous. . . .

"When Don Vernon Gomez got into difficulties he simply 'turned it on' and mowed the Giants down. Cholly the Red Ruffing simply walked out there and overpowered the Polo Grounders."

12. 1969 Orioles

Members of Hall of Fame: 3.

This Oriole club, the first post-World War II team to make our list, was sixth in Games Ahead of Second.

Frank Robinson, the right fielder, who the Orioles had obtained from the Reds in 1965, batted .308 with 32 homers and 100 RBI. Boog Powell, the first baseman, batted .304 with 37 home runs and 121 RBI.

Mark Belanger, who became the Baltimore shortstop in 1968, was outstanding. Brooks Robinson was the brilliant third baseman. He won 11 fielding titles and played in 18 consecutive All-star games. Elrod Hendricks caught.

Screwballer Mike Cuellar, who was obtained from

Houston in 1968, led the Orioles in pitching with a record of 23-11. Dave McNally was 20—7. Jim Palmer was 16—4.

This was the best Baltimore team since 1896 when the Orioles, then in the National League, won 90 and lost 39 behind Hall of Famers Wee Willie Keeler, "Uncle Robbie" Robinson, Hughie Jennings and Joe Kelley.

Murray Chass previewed the Eastern Division champion Orioles' chances in the American League playoff against the Western Division winning Minnesota Twins in the *New York Times* on Oct. 4, 1969:

"BALTIMORE. OCT. 3. The Baltimore Orioles have history on their side, Billy Martin acknowledged today, but he and his Minnesota Twins are more concerned with Mike Cuellar, Boog Powell and the rest of the Orioles. They are the historians, the ones who wrote Baltimore's 1969 baseball history, and they're the ones the Twins will try to overcome for the American League pennant. . . .

"'I'm very impressed with their 109 wins,' said Martin, the [Twins'] rookie manager. . . . 'We know they have a great team - good pitching, good defense and good hitting. . . .'

Arthur Daley commented a week later in the *Times* on the Orioles' playoff sweep and their upcoming series appearance against the New York Mets:

"Most of the [American] League's strength was concentrated in [the Eastern Division] and the natural expectation was that a fierce fight would ensue, one that might go all the way to the wire. But the Birds flew off from the groundlings opposing them.

"By June, they had a 10-game lead and were virtually out of sight. Certainly, they were out of reach as they finished with 109 victories, a total that moved at the same approximate plateau of the fabled Yankee of Murderers' Row distinction. . . .

"However, the Orioles were not yet assured of the American League pennant. According to the new system of preliminary divisional playoffs, they still had to beat the best in the west. . . . They beat the Twins in three straight. . . .

"Now the Orioles will climb into a Baltimore ring against the 'Amazing Mets' starting tomorrow. . . . The Orioles are hereby warned to keep their guards up at all times. . . .

"It is somewhat obvious, but Baltimore is the best team in baseball. It has the same beautiful balance as the old time Yankees of the Ruthian era - expressive hitting, slick defense and overpowering pitching. . . . But the Mets are the hottest team in baseball. . . .

"The first two Baltimore starters, Mike Cuellar and Dave McNally are lefties. The next one, Jim Palmer, is right handed. All three are enormously talented, each ranking at the top of his profession. . . .

"The thing that worries followers of the 'Fantastics' is that there are no holes in the Baltimore batting order. The eighth hitter is Mark Belanger, a fielding phenom at shortstop. . . . This year he is batting .287. In fact, the team averages a solid .265 to .241 for the Mets while Baltimore's home run total is 175 to 109."

The *Times'* Leonard Koppett the next day presented a similar view:

"The Orioles . . . are accepted on all sides as one of the more powerful teams in all baseball history and certainly one of the two or three most impressive squads of the 1960's. Logic should therefore make the Orioles overwhelming favorites and the law of averages should say that Met miracles should not continue indefinitely. The betting line which takes into consideration the emotional preferences by which people are likely to make bets as well as 'objective' factors, has Baltimore favored at 8-5 to take the series."

However, the "miracles" did continue as the Mets captured the series in five games. Arthur Daley commented on this stunning result in the Oct. 17 *Times*:

"What else did you expect? In one final convulsive rupture of the credibility gap, those darlings of destiny, the 'Amazing Mets,' came roaring from behind in their last three turns at bat to win the championship of the world in the Shea Stadium madhouse yesterday.

"From start to finish, this ninth place team of a year ago defied belief. . . . In this series, especially, they made no mistakes after they settled down at the conclusion of a loss in the opener. They then regained their mystique and their magic."

Robert Lipsyte recapped this memorable series in the *Times* the next day:

"The Orioles were under pressure to win because they were considered the best team in baseball while the Mets would be honored merely for suiting up."

So, as in 1954 when a Cleveland Indian team that had won 111 games was upset in a sweep by an underdog New York Giants team, the Orioles - after winning 109 - went down four games to one to another upstart.

13. 1910 Athletics

Members of Hall of Fame: 4.

This was the immortal Connie Mack's first truly great team. Pitcher Chief Bender won 23 and lost 5. Jack Coombs led the league in wins with a record of 31—9 and an ERA of 1.30.

In hitting, the A's were led by their 23-year-old second baseman, Eddie Collins, who batted .322 while driving in 81 runs. Collins who stole 81 bases and was also a superb fielder.

These Athletics placed third in Earned Run Average and sixth in Net Batting Average.

Just about the same players comprised the 1911 Athletics, our 23rd best team of all time.

Before the 1910 World Series between the Athletics and the Chicago Cubs began, the *New York Times* had a former manager of the Chicago White Sox compare the two teams. Fielder A. Jones, who had managed the White Sox in 1908, wrote about the A's great pitchers on Oct. 16, 1910:

"I do know something about Bender, Plank and Coombs and that is that they are three of the best in the business. Not only can they pitch, but they can field their positions, and they are bound to give the Cubs or any other clubs trouble if they are as good as they can be."

On Oct. 21, Fielder commented on the A's team's impressive series' start:

"The Philadelphia Athletics by making it three straight in today's game against the Cubs, practically clinched their title to the world's championship. . . .

"[By the fifth inning], the Athletics, by their great hitting, had forced Chance to retire Reulbach and McIntire and call Pfeister to the rescue. The final score was 12 to 5, but did not indicate the relative ability of the two teams.

"Both the offensive and defensive playing of the Athletics was far superior to that of the Cubs. They were able to hit all kinds of pitching and their aggressive fielding was up to the standard of the two games played on their home grounds. On the other hand, the Cubs weren't able to hit Coombs. . . .

"Jack Barry, Connie Mack's young shortstop, was the

bright light today. The manager of the Athletics, without intending it, has shown in the three games played so far, that his club isn't a one man affair in any particular. His players, particularly in the infield, have shown that everyone of them is a ballplayer.

"In the first game at Philadelphia, Frank Baker was the star. In the second game, the one in which Coombs beat Brown, Collins lived up to the reputation he made in the American League and today Barry got his opportunity and he made good.

"Not only did he field his position perfectly, but he also gave a great exhibition of timely hitting. The fact that he had three two-base hits was not as impressive as the fact that his long hits came when they were needed. Dan Murphy's cleanup hit in the third inning was the one that really settled the result of the game."

The Athletics went on to win the series four games to one.

14. 1912 New York Giants

Members of Hall of Fame: 2.

First baseman Fred Merkle batted .309. Chief Meyers, the Gotham's backstop, was the leading hitter at .358.

On the mound, they were led by Rube Marquard with a record of 26—11. He won 19 straight games and led the league in wins. Christy Mathewson was 23—12.

Hugh S. Fullerton, one of the foremost baseball critics in the country at that time, compared these Giants with the opposing Boston Red Sox (the 15th best team) before the World Series began in the Oct. 7, 1912 *New York Times*:

"Boston's Red Sox ought to win the next world's championship. If the New York Giants win more than two games in the series, I shall cease to believe in dope at all and concede that there is something in baseball beyond the mechanical ability to play the game. . . .

"Unless things break for them all the time, the Giants are beaten. Boston has a better team playing better ball with a better system than that of New York. . . .

"I have reduced the teams to cold figures. On the basis of 100 as absolute perfection in everything, I figure Boston at 69 and New York at 56, a difference so great as to overbalance the element of luck in such a series.

"Boston excels New York at seven of the nine positions. Boston plays better team ball. Boston in its present form has a better pitching staff."

Yet, the series was tight to the finish. On Oct. 16, the *Times* described the Giants' third win:

"New York won the worst played game in the history of the World Series 11 to 4. The victory by the Giants evened up the World Series.

"With the Red Sox unexpectedly thrown back on the defensive, with 'Smoky Joe' Wood beaten, with the team outwitted, outgeneraled [the Sox] are in a panic.

"The betting for the first time favors New York and it looks as if luck may yet carry the Giants forth to the world championship."

This was actually the seventh game. Each team had three wins with one tie (a game called for darkness).

A shocking mistake helped decide the final contest. This report appeared on the *Times'* front page Oct. 17:

"Write in the pages of World Series history the name of Snodgrass. Write it large and black, not as a hero. Truly not.

"Put him level with Merkle who was in such a hurry that he gave away a National League championship. Snodgrass was in such a hurry that he gave away a world championship.

"It was because of Snodgrass' generous muff of an easy fly in the 10th inning that the decisive game in the World Series went to the Boston Red Sox . . . by a score of 3 to 2 instead of to the New York Giants by a score of 2 to 1.

"It is the 10th inning of the eighth game of the series. The score of games is 3 to 3 and the score in this contest is 1 to 1. Mathewson, the veteran, has given the lie to his own announcement that he can never again pitch in such a contest by holding the Red Sox enemy at bay for nine innings in decisive fashion. . . .

"The . . . members of the Boston team have been helpless in the face of his speed and his elusive fadeaway. . . . Their only hope is that Wood, who was done in two innings before, will hold out until the veteran should give way to the strain."

The Giants scored in the top of the 10th to take a 2-1 lead.

The "mountainous" Engle leads off the last half of the 10th. The story continues, "All that Engle can do with the elusive drop served up is to hoist it high between centre and right fields. . . .

"Snodgrass yells 'I've got it' and sets himself. . . . And now the ball settles. It is full and fair in the padded glove of Snodgrass, but he is too eager to toss it to Murray and it dribbles to the ground. Before Snodgrass can hurl the ball to second, Engle is perched there.

"Mathewson . . . is stunned for a moment. . . . It can be seen as he faces Hooper that there is just a bit of uncertainty in his bearing. . . .

"Hooper hits the ball so hard that Snodgrass has to sprint and reach to pull down the liner. . . . For Yerkes he can not put the ball over at all and two Red Sox are on the bases. . . .

"Speaker pops up a high foul near first base and

Merkle, Meyers and Mathewson converge on it with none collected enough to say which shall take it and it drops among them. . . . Speaker, saved by a bungle, hammers the ball hard to right field and Engle is over the plate.

"Lewis stands still while four bad ones pass him and then Gardner steps up and puts all his weight against the ball and it goes far out to Devore - too far for him to stop Yerkes with the winning run."

That same week, the "unsinkable" Titanic sank, and the "unbeatable" Giants lost the series to the Sox, 4 games to 3.

Chapter 10
15th thru 18th: Red Sox, Indians, Cubs and Giants

15. 1912 Red Sox

Members of Hall of Fame: 2.

The Red Sox celebrated their first season in the newly opened Fenway Park by winning the American League pennant.

Center fielder Tris Speaker led the league in home runs that year with 10, batted .383, knocked in 90 runs and stole 52 bases. In pitching, these Red Sox were led by Smokey Joe Wood who led the league in wins with 34 against just five losses.

This team is said to have had the greatest defensive outfield in history made up of Speaker, Duffy Lewis and Harry Hooper. All three covered a great deal of ground and had rifle arms.

Lewis batted in 109 runs.

A *New York Times* account of the World Series appears earlier under the 1912 New York Giants, the 14th-ranked team.

16. 1954 Indians

Members of Hall of Fame: 3.

In 1954, the Cleveland Indians dethroned the New York Yankees, who had won the pennant in each of the five previous years.

This team set an American League record by winning 111 games in 1954. They attracted crowds of more than 80,000 to some games during the season.

The club was fourth in Percentage of Games Won and seventh in Net Earned Run Average.

Only Larry Doby, Dale Mitchell, Jim Hegan, Bob Lemon and Bob Feller were back from the 1948 world champion Indians.

Second baseman Bobby Avila led the league in hitting with a .341 average. Doby, the center fielder and the first black to play in the American League, led the league in homers with 32 and in RBI with 126. Al Rosen, the third baseman, hit .300 with 24 home runs and 102 runs batted in.

Early Wynn and Bob Lemon tied for the most wins in the league. Wynn was 23—11. Lemon was 23—7. Mike Garcia had the best ERA in the league at 2.64. His record was 19—8. Feller, no longer the boy wonder, won 13 and lost 3. Art Houtteman was 15—7. Ray Narleski had 13 saves.

John Drebinger of the *New York Times* on Sept. 27, 1954, analyzed the defenses in the upcoming World Series matching the Indians and New York Giants:

"The 1954 World Series rivals certainly are most evenly matched and as a consequence, this could develop into a thrill-packed series."

Drebinger told how it was difficult to evaluate the teams defensively because of the use of two-platooning to improve the offense.

"Many managers have become addicted to two-platooning because of the successes of Casey Stengel," he commented.

"Mound requirements for a World Series differ significantly from the needs of a successful pennant campaign. For the long 154-game haul, depth is of utmost importance. In a World Series, it is less essential.

"Hence, the mound superiority which at first seems to weigh heavily in the Indians' favor looms less formidable when applied to the brief whirl of the series.

"In the matter of depth, the Indians came up with an extraordinary staff this year. It was perhaps the outstanding single factor that enabled the Tribe to end the five-year reign of the Yankees.

"There were three ace starters, Bob Lemon, Early Wynn and Mike Garcia. And behind them came Bob Feller, who staged an astounding comeback; a vastly improved Art Houtteman and a rejuvenated Hal Newhouser.

"Add to this the splendid relief work of Don Mossi and Ray Narleski, and you have a mound corps that does look foolproof for any sort of competition. . . .

"[But], this edge is shaved down considerably when one holds in mind this is no long haul but a short skirmish. For such an assignment, the Giant staff looks adequate enough. . . .

"At third, . . . Al Rosen, who, handicapped by a succession of injuries, hasn't been quite the player this year that he was in 1953. . . .

"At short, . . . George Strickland has developed into one of the finest glove men to work in the business. . . .

"As for the outfield . . . there is only one Willie Mays and the Giants have him. Willie, unquestionably, is one of the great center fielders of our time. . . .

"He is such a tremendous play maker and possesses such a powerfully accurate arm. . . . The Indians, in Larry Doby, Al Smith, Dave Philley, Wally Westlake and Dave Pope have sound, workmanlike gardeners. . . . But, Mays is in a class by himself.

"Behind the plate, Wes Westrum and Jim Hegan, two

of the best, are a stand-off.

"So, summing it up, while the Indians might be conceded a slight advantage in pitching, the superior overall fielding skill of the Giants should offset this to make it virtually a stand-off on the defense."

Drebinger looked at the offenses the next day in the *Times*:

"Both clubs are going into this series with high-powered offenses.

"For only the third time in World Series history, the two league batting champions will be facing each other. . . . It will be the Giants' Willie Mays against the Indians' Bob Avila. . . .

"The Indians have in Larry Doby the American League's leading home run clouter and run producer. . . .

"The Tribe's really solid man on the offensive still is a fellow named Al Rosen. Injuries may have shackled this slugging third sacker who last year was the unanimous choice for his league's Most Valuable Player award. But Rosen still is a potent man at the bat with an even .300 mark for the year and 24 homers. . . .

"However, the offensive advantage must be granted the Polo Grounders. . . .

"[Al] Lopez is the sound, orthodox leader who plays it close to the vest and according to the book which he knows very well. . . .

"Summing it all up, therefore, we find the two clubs evenly matched."

Sports columnist Arthur Daley wrote with amazing prescience in the *Times* on Sept. 28:

"Perhaps this is merely a hunch . . . the Giants will beat the Indians in the World Series which starts tomorrow. . . .

"The Giants . . . are merely a sound, solid ball club with so much dogged determination that they have an astounding amount of resiliency, perpetually bouncing back and always winning 'the big game,' the one they just had to win. . . .

"Besides, [Giant Manager Leo] Durocher . . . in times of crisis . . . is most psychic. . . . Logic says the Indians should win, but the hunch says the Giants."

It was not a complete surprise then when the Indians were upset in the series losing all four games.

Columnist Daley showed little mercy to the American League pennant winners, now so quickly beaten. On Oct. 3, he wrote:

"A breathless hush fell over the sprawling expanse of the [Cleveland] Municipal Stadium in the ninth inning. . . .

"It was so quiet that you could almost hear a heart break. The Cleveland Indians, proud champions of the American League with a record victory total of 111 games, were down to their last three outs.

"After walking Sam Dente, Johnny Antonelli, with inexorable precision, gathered the outs one, two, three as the mourners watched in stunned and unbelieving silence. The Giants had won the World Series in four straight!

"Even the Polo Grounds tenants . . . seemed to realize that it would have been indecorous to intrude on someone's hour of grief. . . . No one raised his voice or even a grimey fist in jubilation. . . .

"No one spoke even one kind word about the deceased. The Indians died friendless and alone. It was a sad, sad end. Please omit flowers. . . .

"[Casey] Stengel wasn't the only American Leaguer puzzled to the point of bafflement by the behavior of the Indians in this series. It was almost as if they were gazing at a gross caricature of the team they had watched admiringly all during the campaign."

Daley commented further the next day:

"The Cleveland Indians who looked so dreadful in losing to the New York Giants in four straight World Series games were still considerably superior to the Yankees in the regular season. Therefore, the Yankees and the entire American League have to share in the Tribe's disgrace.

"It was a disgrace, too. . . . They played dull, spiritless, maladroit baseball with every hidden weakness horribly exposed. . . .

"One question was being asked all over the map: How could this team score a record 111 victories during the regular campaign and not score even one victory in the World Series?

"The answer is simple. The Tribe murdered everyone on pitching. . . .

"Most teams in the American League averaged approximately one good pitcher apiece. Or we could be generous and double that number. That still isn't enough to match the Indians' strong-armed boys in a three or four-game series."

17. 1907 Cubs

Members of Hall of Fame: 4.

The Cubs won the National League crown for the second consecutive year with essentially the same players who won in 1906.

They were first in Earned Run Average and tied for first in World Series Net among the pennant winners. The club also finished sixth in Percentage of Games Won and tenth in Games Ahead of Second.

First baseman Frank Chance led the team in hitting with .293. Orvie Overall led in pitching with a 23 and 8 record.

The Cubs swept Ty Cobb and the Detroit Tigers in four straight games in the World Series. On Oct. 13,

1907, the *New York Times* reported on the series finale:

"DETROIT, MICH. OCT. 12. The Chicago National League baseball team this afternoon at Bennett Park won the world's championship defeating the Detroit American League team by the score of 2 to 0. It was the fourth successive victory for the Chicago team in as many days. . . .

"It was a disappointing day for the local team in more ways than one. The weather was raw and cold, entirely unfit for baseball, and less than half of the expected 18,000 persons attended the game. The official count . . . was 7,370."

Elsewhere in the *Times* that day this analysis appeared:

"There was no question as to the best team winning. Chicago outplayed, outbatted, outfielded and outgeneraled its opponents."

18. 1905 Giants

Members of Hall of Fame: 2.

After refusing to participate in a World Series in 1904, the Giants' ownership agreed to play the Philadelphia Athletics for the major league crown in 1905.

The Giants led the National League from April 23 to the end of the season.

The great Christy Mathewson, then a 26-year-old graduate of Bucknell University, topped the league in both wins and ERA. His record was 31—8 losses; with an ERA of 1.27.

Almost the same players made up the 1904 Giants, the 20th best team of all time.

On Oct. 8, 1905, the *New York Times* looked ahead to the series:

"With the National League championship settled for the second time in succession in favor of the New York team more than a week ago and a similar honor going to the Philadelphia Athletics in the American League on Friday last, the next important event before the closing of the season will be the meeting of the two teams in a series, best four of seven, for the world championship beginning tomorrow in Philadelphia.

"This fixture has excited the patrons of the game probably to a greater extent than any other event that has occurred in the history of baseball.

"That the coming contest will be fought out between the teams that are justly entitled to the distinction cannot be questioned.

"In a season that surpassed all others in brilliancy and in attendance, the New York National League team under the management of John J. McGraw showed itself to be points stronger than any other team in the league. . . .

"That pitching will cut a big swath in the series is confidently believed by all competent judges. . . .

"The supporters of the champion New Yorks point to the brilliant achievements of Mathewson this year and believe that he is without an equal as a pitcher. . . .

"The New Yorks will [also] present Joe McGinnity, the 'Iron Man,' who while not being quite so successful as last year, may be considered a dangerous factor; Ames, Taylor, and the left-handed Wiltse.

"The New Yorks have an advantage in batting and three of their men - Donlin, McGann and Bresnahan - have placed above the .300 mark."

With the series in progress, the *Times* reported on Oct. 13:

"In head work, New York has surpassed Philadelphia and that tells the story of the Giants' conquests. [The Giants led two games to one.]

"In the aggregate, a eulogy of today's play would

point without discrimination to the nine men who did the work as a whole, but individually, only to that professor of occult speed and pretzel curve, Christie Mathewson.

"When the Factoryville baseball genius won his game on Monday, Philadelphia admired. Tonight, they wondered.

"Considering his record for the 18 innings he has officiated, it is not astonishing. During that performance, he allowed only nine hits and no contender got beyond second base.

"His twirling today was mainly a fan-fest and at all times in the situation he was a complete master."

Page 1 of the Oct. 15 *Times* brought news of the Giants' series triumph:

"The Giants, the most intelligent, the quickest, the strongest and grittiest combination of baseball players that have ever represented this city in any league, demonstrated beyond opportunity, quibble or claim, their paramount superiority over anything extant in diamond life of today by winning the fifth and deciding game of the world's championship series by the score of 2 to 0.

"The crowd, in the neighborhood of 27,000 people, saw the battle, and a battle it was, to cheer the baseball heart and satisfy the innermost cravings of the rooter's mind. . . .

"At no time during the contest were the Giants in danger and at all times were they masters. . . .

"And be it recorded right here that New York possesses the pitching marvel of the century. Christie Mathewson, the Giant slabman who made the world championship possible for New York, may be designated as the pitching wonder of all baseball records. . . .

"His almost superhuman accomplishment during the

series which closed yesterday, will stand as the mark for all pitchers of the future.

"In the three victories in which he presided, he twirled 27 innings. During that series, he allowed not a single run. No Athletic even reached third base.

"He was touched for only a total of 15 hits. . . . He allowed only one pass to first, hit only a single batsman and struck out 16 men.

The Giants captured the World Series from the Athletics four games to one.

Chapter 11
19th thru 22nd: Cards, Giants, Dodgers and Pirates

19. 1942 Cardinals

Members of Hall of Fame: 2.

The old "Gashouse Gang" had scattered, but General Manager Branch Rickey assembled yet another St. Louis powerhouse from his vaunted farm system.

Rookie Stan Musial batted .315. Hustling Enos Slaughter, the right fielder, led the team in hitting at .318, while Harry Walker batted .314.

Mort Cooper led the league in wins with 22 against 7 losses. He also led the league in ERA. Rookie Johnny Beazley was also a 20-game winner.

On Sept. 29, 1942, an unnamed *New York Times* "staff correspondent" previewed the upcoming World Series between the Cardinals and the New York Yankees:

"When an entry comes roaring into a series as have the Cards, winning 43 of their last 53 games while losing only nine and tying one to overcome a 10 game deficit in the last seven weeks, form comparisons can be little more than worthless.

"And so, while the average baseball observer may favor the Yankees, as he invariably has done in the past, he must take into account the amazing dash of Billy Southworth's spectacular youngsters.

"On the defense, although this is the Cards' forte, there seems little to choose. . . .

"The Redbirds' pitching staff is perhaps the most impressive that any National League club has brought into the series in many years. Topped by the two crack right handers, Mort Cooper and Johnny Beazley, two superb lefties in Ernie White and Max Lanier, not to overlook Howie Pollet, and backed by two capable relief flingers, Howard Krist and Murry Dickson, they are mostly youngsters but mighty good and they have a fine catcher in Walker Cooper.

"The infield, starring the rangy Marty Marion at short, is a closely knit quartet and the outfield, defensively, knows few equals and certainly no superiors.

"Terry Moore has been one of the greatest ball hawks in a half a dozen years. The rookie Stan Musial already has shown promise of running Moore a close second. And Enos Slaughter is more than passing fair in right.

"On the offensive, however, we once again find that decided pull toward the Yanks. They have the long ball hitters. . . .

"Not that the Cards do not have a spectacular offensive of their own. Theirs has been remarkable. It works with lightning speed, taking advantage of every break and often making its own . . . breaks. . . .

"Summing up, analysts look for a low-scoring series but with that extra inning power giving the Yanks the edge."

The series, however, went only five games and the Cardinals were the upset winners. On the *Times'* front page Oct. 6 was a description of the deciding game:

"In the ninth inning of yesterday's fifth game of the 1942 World Series, with a crowd of 59,052 looking on while two fine hurlers, old Red Ruffing and young Johnny Beazley were locked in a two-all tie, George [Whitey] Kurowski, a youngster, just one year out of the minors, bashed a home run into the densely packed stands of the Yankee Stadium.

"It streaked through the mist of a leaden grayish afternoon and on the wings of that shot, which came with a runner on the base paths, there came to an end one of the most remarkable World Series dynasties baseball has ever known.

"For with that blow, the St. Louis Cardinals brought down Joe McCarthy's mighty Yankees 4 to 2 to win their fourth straight encounter.

"It bagged the world championship for Billy Southworth's National League champions four games to one and completed the most amazing upset in series history since 1914. . . .

"They were two to one underdogs as they squared away against the powerful Yanks who had not been vanquished in World Series conflict in 16 years."

The Yanks had not lost a World Series since 1926 when they lost to another Cardinal team, led by Rogers Hornsby.

20. 1904 Giants

Members of Hall of Fame: 3.

The Giants had *two* 30-game winners in 1904! Joe McGinnity led the league in both wins and ERA. He won 35 games and lost 8. Christy Mathewson was 33—12.

The team was tenth in both Percentage of Games Won and in Earned Run Average.

Because of a dispute, there was no World Series in 1904. The *New York Times* gave the Giants' view of this situation on Oct. 7, 1904:

"Both John T. Brush, president, and John J. McGraw, manager of the New York baseball club, made it clear last night that there would be no games played between their club and the winners of the American League pennant for the world's championship, held by the Boston Americans. . . .

"Manager McGraw issued this statement: 'I want to go clearly, emphatically on record. . . . The people of New York have been kind enough to give me some credit for bringing the pennant to New York and if there is any just blame and criticism for the club's action in protecting that highly prized honor, the blame should rest on my shoulders, not Mr. Brush's. . . .

'When I came to New York three years ago, the team was in last place. Since that time, . . . I have hoped to bring the pennant to New York. . . . Now that the New York team has won this honor, I for one will not stand to see it tossed away like a rag. The pennant means something to me. It is the first I have ever won.

'It means something to my players and they are with me in my stand. We never stopped until we clinched the pennant even though it did rob the game of the interest of a pennant race. The club never complained.

'While the play was hot, we played to thousands. After the race was won, we played to hundreds. . . . If we didn't sacrifice our race in our own league to the box office, we certainly are not going to put in jeopardy the highest honor in baseball simply for the box office inducement.

'If the National League should see fit to place postseason games on the same plane as championship games and surround them with the same protection and safeguards as championship games, then and not until then will I ever take part in them.'"

What all of this really meant is hard to tell, but we do know that McGraw and his Giants *did* win the World Series in 1905.

21. 1953 Dodgers

Members of Hall of Fame: 4.

The 1953 Brooklyn Dodgers were led by right fielder Carl Furillo who batted a league leading .344. Duke Snider in center batted .336. Jackie Robinson, now in right field, batted .329. Roy Campanella, the catcher, led the league in runs batted in with 142. Snider had 126 RBI and first baseman Gil Hodges had 122.

Carl Erskine led the pitching staff with a record of 20—6. Russ Meyer, Billy Loes, Preacher Roe and reliever Clem Labine had double figure win totals.

Pee Wee Reese, Billy Cox, rookie Jim Gilliam and Hodges gave the Dodgers an airtight infield.

The team placed second in both Net Runs and Net Slugging Average and tenth in Runs.

Arthur Daley of the *New York Times* on Sept. 28, 1953, wrote of the coming World Series against the crosstown Yankees:

"It could very well be that the coming World Series will be decided in left field. The Dodgers have a left fielder named Jackie Robinson, a new boy on the job.

"Jackie is a whale of a ballplayer but he never played the outfield in the big leagues and he never has played there in Yankee Stadium during a World Series when the purple haze and the tricky sun play pranks."

John Drebinger the same day compared the Dodgers with their American League foe on offense in the *Times*:

"A couple of mishaps have reduced two Dodger hitters to unknown quantities. Carl Furillo and Gil Hodges are the unknown quantities. . . .

"Both came down with injuries that threw them out of action and off stride within the last three weeks of the regular season. Both are expected to play.

"Back in August . . . it was the conviction in this corner . . . that the Flatbush Flock would bring a preponderance of power into the series, so much so, in fact, that it couldn't help but win. . . .

"Along in May, Hodges started teeing off and he kept going all summer and until [he was hurt], he was hitting a robust .303 with 31 homers and 120 runs batted in.

"Furillo, at the time he suffered a finger fracture in his rather senseless brawl with Leo Durocher, was leading the league with .344.

"Happily for the Dodgers, their power does not rest wholly on these two. In fact, they are only a part of the grand offensive that flattened the best of the pitching in the National League.

"The top slugger is Roy Campanella who has enjoyed a spectacular year. The 'Round Man of Flatbush' is a devastating hitter, capable of wrecking any game with a long ball.

"Only a stripe behind him comes Duke Snider who almost single- handedly won the Series for the Dodgers last year. . . .

"Then there is Jackie Robinson, still one of the most consistent hitters the game has ever seen. . . .

"Add to this an exceptionally adroit batsman in Pee Wee Reese and you have with Furillo and Hodges at or near their best, a formidable battlefront that would tax the most skillful pitching.

"The Dodgers, with or without Furillo and Hodges at their best, must be given the edge on the offense."

Drebinger looked at the opposing defenses on Sept. 29:

"Chuck Dressen [Dodger manager] hasn't quite the staff to match the Bombers in balance and depth. However, . . . Chuck has revealed himself as a masterful handler of pitchers. . . .

"This year, he comes to the mark with that added starter, Russ Meyer, whose 15-5 record just about sewed up the pennant for the Dodgers this season. Also, Carl Erskine, a 20-game winner who, with this added year of experience, has increased vastly in stature, plus the still wily southpaw, Preacher Roe ... and the fireballing youngsters, right-handed Billy Loes, and southpaw Johnny Podres.

"Clem Labine, Bob Milliken, Ben Wade and Jim Hughes have given Chuck satisfactory service [from the bullpen]. ...

"The outfields balance out fairly well, what with Gene Woodling's advantage over Jackie Robinson in left being more than offset by Duke Snider's superiority over Mickey Mantle in center.

"The infields ... are virtually a stand-off and behind the plate each side is equipped with the best catcher in its league, Yogi Berra and Roy Campanella.

Drebinger predicted the Yanks would win in seven games. The Yanks actually did it in six.

On Sept. 30, Arthur Daley made his choice in the *Times*:

"The Yankees had already completed their 18-game winning streak and had a stranglehold on the pennant while the Brooks were still floundering and were still trying frantically to get straightened away.

"But, then, Brooklyn became truly impressive. All the pieces in Dressen's jigsaw puzzle fell neatly into place. Junior Gilliam became a gifted second baseman and Jackie Robinson, wonder that he is, an accomplished outfielder. Gil Hodges, Duke Snider and Carl Furillo joined Roy Campanella as prodigious hitters.

"The pitching rotation smoothed out ... And, what hitters there were! Furillo won the batting championship with Snider fourth, Robinson seventh and Campy tenth while Hodges was also in the .300-plus bracket. Campy led the league in runs batted in. Campy also hit

41 homers, Snider 42 and Hodges 31. The Brooklyn team belted a near-record 208 homers. . . .

"To top everything else, the Dodgers clinched the championship earlier than any other National League team in history. Two days later the Yankees clinched their flag. . . .

"In cold statistics, it must seem that the Dodgers have the edge. But, there is another phase to baseball . . . 'the intangibles.'

"The Yankees have the intangibles. . . . The hesitant choice here is the Yankees."

Just one week later, Daley commented on the just completed World Series, which his "hesitant choice" had taken four games to two:

"The greatest of all Dodger teams - or so it was labelled - couldn't do a doggone bit better than a slew of lesser teams. The Yankees, as is their habit, won the World Series.

"In one respect, it was like taking candy from a baby. Tease the brat slightly and tantalize him, then jerk the confection from his sticky grasp."

There are other newspaper accounts of this World Series under the 29th best team, the 1953 Yankees.

22. 1909 Pirates

Members of Hall of Fame: 2.

Shortstop Honus Wagner, then one of the best players in major league baseball, led the league in batting for the fourth straight year, with .339. He also led the league in RBI with 100. The Dutchman also was outstanding on the base paths and brilliant as a shortstop with his big hands, long reach and strong throwing arm.

The pitching staff was led by Vic Willis with a 22—11 record and Howie Camnitz at 25—6.

The Pirates were third in Percentage of Games Won and fourth in Earned Run Average.

A look ahead at the upcoming World Series against the Detroit Tigers appeared in the sports pages of the *New York Times* on Oct. 8, 1909:

"PITTSBURGH, PA. OCT 7. Detroit, the American League champions, and Pittsburgh, the winner of the National League pennant, will play here tomorrow the opening game of the series to decide the baseball championship of the world for 1909.

"It will be Detroit's third attempt in as many years to win the greatest honors in organized baseball as Hughie Jennings' champions have been defeated by the Chicago Nationals in the last two world series.

"Pittsburgh has not had an opportunity of contesting for the world's championship since 1903 when it won the National League pennant and was defeated by the Boston Americans in the big series. . . .

"Both Managers Fred Clarke and Jennings will send the men they consider their strongest at present to do the pitching. Jennings said he would probably use George Mullin, his husky and reliable veteran, while Clarke is planning to use Charles Adams, the man who came from the Louisville American Association team at the beginning of this season and made a phenomenal record with Pittsburgh. . . .

"Frank O'Loughlin of the American League and J. E. Johnstone of the National League will umpire tomorrow."

The series proved raucous. From the Oct. 14 *Times*:

"PITTSBURGH. OCT. 13. The National Baseball Commission today announced that it had fined Miller of Pittsburgh $50 for his conduct in yesterday's World Series game and a penalty of $25 was inflicted on Donovan of Detroit for his actions which caused Umpire Klem to send them from the field. The fining of Manager Clarke, Gibson, Leach and Camnitz for their actions in Monday's game makes six fines that have been inflicted in the last two games.

"Ty Cobb, the star right fielder of the Detroit team, did not accompany his teammates on the National Commission's special train last night because of his desire to avoid Cleveland. Manager Jennings of Detroit received information that the Cleveland authorities intended to arrest Cobb as he passed through Cleveland in the special train.

"Cobb had trouble with a hotel watchman in Cleveland recently and it was reported to Jennings that an indictment for felonious assault had been brought against Cobb by the Grand Jury. Cobb came from Detroit to Pittsburgh by way of Buffalo and did not arrive until long after his teammates."

The Pirates went on to win the series and their fans were ecstatic as the *Times* reported Oct. 17:

"PITTSBURGH, PA. OCT. 16. Pandemonium reigned here tonight. Pittsburgh was turned over to the baseball enthusiasts who wildly celebrated the victory of the Pittsburgh Baseball Club today and the winning of the world's championship. Streetcar traffic was practically abandoned on the main thoroughfares downtown and the business centres of the surrounding suburbs rivaled the main streets of this city in the noise and crowds. . . .

"Pictures of Babe Adams, the pitcher who three times defeated Detroit, were displayed on many of the stores and were carried by the fans in the parade.

"Although Pittsburgh has won the National League pennant four times, this is the first time the city has secured the world's championship, their first tries for that honor being unsuccessful."

The deciding game was described in the *Times* the same day:

"DETROIT. OCT. 16. Pittsburgh won the world's baseball championship at Bennett Park today by defeating Detroit by the overwhelming score of 8-0 in the seventh and decisive game of one of the greatest battles ever fought for the world's title.

"This gives the National League champions the victory by a count of four games to three.

"This is the third successive defeat of the American League champions in the World Series . . . the Chicago team having defeated Detroit in 1907 and 1908.

"To Charles Adams, the phenomenal young pitcher formerly of the Louisville American Association team, belongs the lion's share of the credit for the victory and his wonderful pitching has crowded Wagner, Leach, Clarke and the other Pittsburgh stars into the background.

"Today's victory was his third of the series and he held Detroit safely throughout the entire game. He allowed but six hits and in only one inning - the fourth - did Detroit get more than one safety.

"Adams allowed only one base on balls and in four innings he retired the hard-hitting American Leaguers in one-two-three order.

"The crowd was a distinct disappointment as there were only 17,562 paid admissions."

Chapter 12
23rd thru 26th: A's, Mets and Yanks Twice

23. 1911 Athletics

Members of Hall of Fame: 4.

The Athletics won a second straight pennant for Manager Connie Mack.

Second baseman Eddie Collins led the team in hitting with .365. (That year Ty Cobb hit .420 for the Tigers.) Third baseman Frank "Home Run" Baker batted .344 and led the league with 11 round-trippers.

Also in the Athletics' "$100,000 infield" were first baseman Stuffy McInnis and shortstop Jack Barry. McInnis batted .321 and Barry hit .265.

The team placed sixth in Net Batting Average among the pennant winners.

The pitching staff was led by Jack Coombs with 28 wins against 12 losses, topping the American League in wins. Eddie Plank was 23—8.

It took six games before Connie Mack's "White Elephants" could dispatch the New York Giants in the World Series, but they took the final contest convincingly. From the Oct. 27, 1911 *New York Times*:

"SPECIAL TO THE NEW YORK TIMES. PHILADELPHIA. OCT. 26. The baseball pageant of 1911 ended at Shibe Park today with the Athletics intoxicated with victory rolling around the base paths in Philadelphia for the second time in the wildest tally carnival the World Series has ever known.

"The Giants, the National League title holders, were riddled by a fusillade of stinging hits which fell in a shower all over the field and cost them a humiliating defeat by a score of 13-2.

"The deciding game was a rout which made the proud Manhattan team look like minor league tail enders.

"Three pitchers - Ames, Wiltse and Marquard - were flogged relentlessly in the mad dash the Athletics made to wind up the series and retain the highest baseball honors which they batted away from the Chicago Cubs a year ago.

"The New York team, which looked to be such a stubborn band of fighters in the bitter fray at the Polo Grounds on Tuesday, collapsed without even a dying struggle and was battered to pieces by a driving attack which left not even the slightest shadow of a doubt about the supremacy of the American Leaguers.

"It was the veteran Redman flinger, Bender, who again faced the Giants and held them under his spell. The Chippewa allowed only four hits and was deadly effective at all times. . . .

"Bender is the biggest man of his tribe tonight and at some far-off reservation when they get the news the Aborigines will pass the news from wigwam to wigwam and the squaws will tell the little papooses that if they grow up and be good Indians, maybe some day they will be like the great Chief Bender and become heap fine flingers.

"In the fourth, [the Giants] blew up like a lot of schoolboys and after that the game was nothing more than a procession of Athletics around the bases. The Giants were busy watching the parade of runs cross the plate for two hours.

"The seventh inning was a game of "one ol' cat" with the Mackmen jabbing the service of southpaw Wiltse to all uninhabited corners of the meadow.

"Six hits off "Hooks" crowded five runs across and then, McGraw's hope, [Rube Marquard], the National League pitching sensation, went in wild as a hog and the inning produced a total of seven runs and as many hits for the enemy.

"A crowd of 20,000 saw the fun and joined in a hilarious revel over the unlooked for destruction of the New York team. The Giants were completely outplayed in every feature of baseball in this series.

"There is no question about which is the better team. The Athletics are a troupe of clouters far superior to the Giants. The Mack twirlers, Bender, Coombs and Plank were far and away better than the McGraw staff. The Athletics fielding was faster, snappier and more brilliant than the best New York could show.

"As soon as the last man was out this afternoon, McGraw rushed over to the Philadelphia bench and shook Connie Mack's extended hand. Then Mack grinned and said, 'That's squaring ourselves for that trimming in 1905.'

"This is the longest interview Mack has given out during the series. He is a quaint humorist, Mack is.

"With Bender mowing the Giants down one after another and with his team miles ahead, the Athletic manager sent out Plank, Morgan and Krause to warm up. That was rubbing it in and all the Giants could do was sit on their bench and growl. . . .

"Deep-dyed New York rooters sat back in their seats and laughed with the natives in the seventh when the merry-go-round started. The game was a joke.

"The rising generation of William Penn's town will tell their children and children's children about the time way back in 1911 when the fighting Giants of McGraw invaded the Quaker City in quest of the world's baseball title and how the haughty New Yorkers were snuffed out."

Giant pitcher Rube Marquard conceded the Athletics' superiority in a *Times'* article Oct. 27:

"Well, the series has been won and by the best team. We have been up against some ball team, believe me, and we freely admit it.

"Defeat is always bitter but we were fairly and squarely beaten and there isn't a Giant who is not willing to say so. . . . The Athletics beat us in all departments of the game - pitching, batting and fielding - and the last game was a deluge. . . .

"The Athletics are the best team in the world. There is no doubt about it. . . . As a team, we have never been up against better pitching in a series. . . .

"It was the pitching that won the championship. . . . Not one of the Athletics twirlers needed relief except Coombs in the last game in New York and I am told that his injury in that game was serious."

24. 1986 Mets

Members of Hall of Fame: 0.

This, the most recent team to make the Top 30, finished second in the Games Ahead of Second category.

Bob Ojeda led the pitching staff with an 18—5 record. Dwight Gooden was next with a mark of 17—6 and Ron Darling went 15—6. (The Mets had three of the five top pitchers in the NL in ERA.)

Keith Hernandez, first base, led the team in hitting with .310 average. *He* led the league in walks with 94. (Hernandez has been called the best fielding first baseman of all time by one writer.) Wally Backman, second base, batted .320.

In the *New York Times* of Oct. 7, 1986, as the World Series neared, the Mets were appraised by Dave Anderson:

"Over the season, the Mets proved to be the best team in baseball by far - they won 108 games. . . .

"The Mets were expected to win the National League East and they did. . . .

"'The key is our leadoff guys,' [Manager Davey] Johnson said. 'We know we're going to get some hits from Hernandez, Carter and Strawberry and if Dykstra and Backman are on base, we'll get runs.'"

A scouting report by Roger Craig, then manager of the San Francisco Giants, appeared in the Oct. 17 *Times*:

"The World Series will be played by two clubs with great offensive power, but the Mets are better balanced than the [Boston] Red Sox and have better pitching. . . . Pitching wins. . . .

"The Red Sox and the Mets are two clubs with somewhat similar managers, men who like to sit back and wait for the big inning. They like to force things. They are both somewhat low-key in nature. . . .

"But Davey Johnson has the edge in the series because of the pitching, principally in the bullpen. A sizable edge and that should be decisive in a short series.

"You look at the Dwight Goodens, the Bob Ojedas, the Ron Darlings, the Roger McDowells. Awesome.

"Their staff has more versatility than the Red Sox have and that is where baseball games are usually won.

"But, beyond the pitching, the Mets have balance in every direction.

"They have good power, Gary Carter, Darryl Strawberry, guys who can get the ball out of the park. They have speed, Lenny Dykstra and Wally Backman and right at the top of their lineup.

"They have excellent reserves. They have dominant

pitching and they have a bullpen that's extraordinary. . . .

"Pitching and balance: those are the Mets' strengths. Those are the strengths you need to survive."

A tight series ended in a Met seventh-game triumph. From Ira Berkow's report in the *Times* of Oct. 28:

"So the champs were the 'bad guys,' a team that so many fans and players around the country had taken a dislike to. They were called the 'arrogant,' 'blustery,' and 'obnoxious' Mets. . . .

"It began with Johnson [Mets' manager] in spring training saying that his team was so strong it was going to 'dominate.' . . .

"Well, they won their division by 21 1/2 games, but they fought hard to win the pennant over the Astros and the World Series came down to a phenomenal comeback in game six and a rousing triumph in the finale.

"'It wasn't easy,' said Johnson, referring now to the World Series, 'and we beat a formidable foe.' . . .

"Though, in the World Series they did the unthinkable, if not the impossible, having lost the first two games of the series at home and then coming back to win in seven."

The Mets scored three runs in the sixth inning of the seventh game to tie the score before going on to win the game 8-5.

25. 1942 Yankees

Members of Hall of Fame: 2.

The Yanks won their sixth pennant in seven years in 1942.

Joe Gordon, second baseman, batted .322. Joe DiMaggio batted .305 and had 21 homers. Left fielder Charlie Keller had 26 homers.

Pitcher Ernie Bonham was 21 and 5. Spud Chandler, Hank Borowy, Red Ruffing and Lefty Gomez were also on the pitching staff.

Some of the things said about the 1942 World Series may be found in the report on the 1942 Cardinals, the 19th best team of all time.

On Sept. 29, 1942, an article in the sports pages of the *New York Times* evaluated the Yankees' chances against the St. Louis Cardinals in the World Series:

"And so, while the average baseball observer may favor the Yankees, as he invariably has done in the past, he must take into account the amazing dash of Billy Southworth's spectacular youngsters.

"On the defense, although this is the Cards' forte, there seems little to choose. . . .

"Joe McCarthy again is coming in with a high-powered and extensive pitching staff boasting five top flight starters in Ernie Bonham, Charlie Ruffing, Spud Chandler, Atley Donald and the freshman star, Hank Borowy.

"If there is any flaw here it lies only in the absence of an ace left hander, due to the fading of Lefty Gomez and the arm ailment of Marius Russo and in the slight falling off of Johnny Murphy's relief work. . . .

"And behind the plate there is still the matchless Bill Dickey.

"The infield . . . is as airtight as ever with Joe Gordon, greatest of modern second sackers, and the agile Phil Rizzuto, the key of a great double play combination.

"In the outfield, there is the still flawless Joe DiMaggio flanked by two steady workmen in Charlie Keller and Roy Cullenbine, whose work since replacing Tommy Henrich, has been more than adequate.

"On the offensive, however, we once again find that decided pull toward the Yanks. They have the long-ball hitters in DiMaggio, Keller, Gordon and Dickey, also

Cullenbine, all capable of breaking up any low scoring game, and that well might be the decisive edge. . . .

"And the Yankees are one outfit that never gives the other side encouragement with letdowns. . . .

"[Manager] McCarthy . . . is an old hand at World Series play. Since 1932, Joe has been in six, winning them all. . . .

"Summing up, analysts look for a low scoring series but with that extra hitting power giving the Yanks the edge."

John Drebinger gave his view in the *Times* the next day:

"Small wonder, then that the Yanks rule again strong favorites. The odds against their chances . . . are 9 to 20 for the series."

Times sports columnist John Kieran added his opinion Sept. 30:

"But the two gents that Yankee rooters really are counting on are Jolting Joe DiMaggio and Killer Keller. Neither one has the batting average that was expected of him this year, but they slapped out plenty of homers and drove in flocks of runs."

In a stunning upset, however, the Cardinals prevailed in five games. John Drebinger described the final, clinching Cardinal win on the front page of the Oct. 6 *Times*:

"In the ninth inning of yesterday's fifth game of the 1942 World Series, with a crowd of 69,052 looking on while two fine hurlers, old Red Ruffing and young Johnny Beazley, were locked in a 2-all tie, George (Whitey) Kurowski, a youngster just one year out of the minors, bashed a home run into the densely packed stands of the Yankee Stadium.

"It streaked through the mist of a leaden gray afternoon and on the wings of that shot, which came with a runner on the base paths, there came to an end one of the most remarkable World Series dynasties baseball has ever known.

"For with that blow, the St. Louis Cardinals brought down Joe McCarthy's mighty Yankees, 4 to 2, to win their fourth straight encounter. It bagged the world's championship for Billy Southworth's National League champions, four games to one, and completed the most amazing upset in series history since 1914, when the miracle Braves bowled over Connie Mack's heavily favored Athletics."

Times' columnist Kieran writing the same day also was shocked by the outcome:

"It's lucky that there were nearly 70,000 witnesses to the tragedy in the Bronx yesterday or the facts would be hard to believe. The clattering Cardinals, scampering through the dripping fog that enveloped the field, beat the great Yankee team for the fourth straight time and pulled down the curtain on an astonishing series."

26. 1941 Yankees

Members of Hall of Fame: 4.

After finishing just two games out of first in 1940, the Yanks won their fifth pennant in six years in 1941. Their 17-game victory margin was tenth largest in the Games Ahead of Second category.

Joe DiMaggio hit in 56 straight games, batted .357 and had a league leading 125 RBI and 30 home runs. (Ted Williams hit .406 that year.) Rookie Phil Rizzuto at shortstop batted .307. Charlie Keller had 122 runs batted in and 33 homers. Right fielder Tommy Henrich had 31 homers.

Red Ruffing led the pitchers with a record of 15 and 6. Lefty Gomez was 15 and 5. Johnny Murphy led the league with 15 saves.

John Drebinger analyzed the defenses of the Yankees and the Brooklyn Dodgers, their rival in the upcoming World Series, in the *New York Times* on Sept. 29, 1941:

"For as one examines the defensive equipment of the two clubs it becomes strikingly apparent that each will enter the conflict holding a powerful hand in one of the two major phases of defensive play - pitching and fielding.

"To the Dodgers must be conceded the advantage in pitching so far as World Series requirements are concerned. But when you take in the eight remaining positions and consider the defensive qualifications of the two units as a whole, the Yankees just as assuredly hold the edge.

"This, of course, does not mean that the American League champions are coming up to the mark with a weak and uncertain mound corps such as the Tigers brought into the [World Series] fray last October. On the contrary, Manager Joe McCarthy during the past season has directed and manipulated a most remarkable battery of flingers and one which played a vital part in the Yanks' runaway pennant victory.

"It was a staff amazingly well balanced in veterans and youngsters and doubly fortified with a preponderance of material which alone enabled the two old right and left bowers, Charlie Ruffing and Lefty Gomez, to contribute so well to the Yanks' victory column. They always received ample rest between starts and at no time were they ever placed under any undue strain.

"This was because McCarthy had assembled one of the largest groups of first-class hurlers ever seen on a pennant winner. In all, the Yankee skipper won his league race with seven recognized starting pitchers, and all seven are still available for the series. They are, in addition to

Ruffing and Gomez, Chandler, Bonham, Donald, Breuer, and the left-handed Marius Russo. Add to this the eminent relief specialist, Johnny Murphy, and you have as strong a staff for a 154-game pennant campaign as any club could possibly desire. There were no twenty-game winners in the cast, but it needed none. The opposition never got a rest. They uniformly looked at first-class Yankee pitching from May to September. . . .

"[However], World Series competitions have usually gone to the side which dominated the show with a compact staff headed by two standout aces. . . .

"And such a cast is what the Dodgers are bringing to the 1944 classic.

"However, while pitching is a recognized dominant factor in series warfare, the eight other positions also become vitally important when weighing a club's defensive strength. And here the Yanks flash well ahead of their rivals.

"Individually, the Dodgers compare favorably in only two positions. At first . . . and at second. . . . But on the left wing of the infield, the Yanks are well ahead with the incredible Rizzuto at short and the dependable Rolfe at third ranking above Reese and Lavagetto or Riggs. And behind the plate Owen must give way to Dickey who still ranks as one of the great catchers of all time.

"In the outfield, the Yankee advantage is even more pronounced. Reiser, Brooklyn's rookie sensation of the year, has done an amazing job in center. But this still leaves him far behind the flawless Joe DiMaggio. . . . Similarly, Henrich holds a decisive edge over Walker . . . and in left, Keller . . . must be rated above Joe Medwick."

Drebinger wrote again about the two teams the next day:

"The Yankees are still popularly called the Bronx

BABE RUTH of the '27 Yankees. . . "Superman of the game"

JOE DIMAGGIO of the '39 Yankees. . . Batted .381 with 30 home runs

LEFTY GROVE of the '29 Athletics . . . Won 20 games and led the league in ERA

CHICAGO NATIONAL LEAGUE BALL CLUB 1906

M. BROWN.   A. HOFMAN   C.G.WILLIAMS   O.OVERALL   E.REULBACH   J. KLING
J. GESSLER.   J. TAYLOR.   H. STEINFELDT. J.MCCORMICK F.CHANCE.   J.SHECKARD. P. MORAN   F.SCHULTE
J.FEISTER.   C.LUNDGREN.   T.WALSH.   J. EVERS   J.SLAGLE.   J.TINKER.

1906 CHICAGO CUBS. . . Featured DP combo of Tinker to Evers to Chance

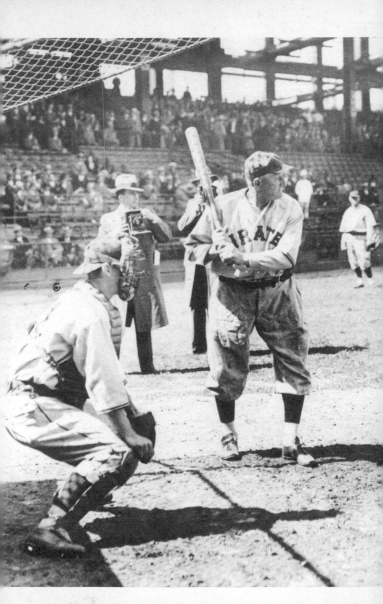

HONUS WAGNER **of the '02 Pirates**... Played three positions and led league in RBI

STAN MUSIAL **of the '44 Cards**. . . Stan "the Man" led the Cards in batting

BROOKS ROBINSON **of the '69 Orioles.** . . May be the best field-ing third baseman ever

CONNIE MACK (left), manager of the '16 Athletics... Managed 4 of the best and 4 of the worst teams of all time

Bombers. As a matter of fact, there is nothing so explosive or dynamic about their attack, and there hasn't been for a number of years. They still lead their league in home runs, but into this series they are carrying no such devastating offense as crushed the Cubs in 1932 or 1938 and the Giants in 1936-1937.

"Their attack today . . . is more the compact, efficient sort which seems to synchronize beautifully with the defense. Throughout the weeks of their sensational mid-summer drive, when they ripped their league apart, the Yanks seemed to win games with almost effortless ease. . . .

"The Yankees' attack, of course, is centered in their matchless Joe DiMaggio and the rugged Charlie Keller. DiMaggio is one of the great batters of all time, a deadly consistent hitter whose phenomenal 56-game streak set the Yanks on fire and presently burned up the rest of the league. He finished as the circuit's leading run driver. . . .

"Keller . . . is a powerful, long-range clouter. . . . Not far behind Keller come Joe Gordon and Tommy Henrich. . . .

"Bill Dickey, no longer the home run slugger of old, still packs a dangerous punch. The same for Red Rolfe. Phil Rizzuto packs no power at all. . . . But he has just completed his first season in the majors with a .308 batting mark, gets on base a great deal and so plays an invaluable part in the general scheme of the attack.

"Summed up, the Yanks perhaps still show a slight edge by reason of their longer range. . . .

"On the managerial side, the advantage must go to the Yanks, if for no other reason than Joe McCarthy's far greater experience.

"McCarthy's managerial edge, plus that indefinable commodity known as 'class' should make the Yankees the choice. But we look to an intensely interesting and dramatic series that is almost certain to go to six games."

Drebinger picked the winner correctly, but the Yankees only took five games to achieve victory. The sportswriter filed this report on Oct. 7 after the final contest:

"Sweeping irresistibly toward their goal in a manner to which they long since had become accustomed, the Yankees vanquished the Dodgers once more at Ebbets Field yesterday and, with this victory, achieved by a score of 3 to 1, again established themselves as undisputed champions of the universe. The triumph gave Joe McCarthy's invincible Bronx Bombers the 1941 World Series four games to one.

"In striking contrast to Sunday's cyclonic struggle, which saw the Yanks bludgeon their way out of the shadows of defeat, with a four-run blast that exploded in the wake of Mickey Owen's imperishable error, the end came quietly yesterday at 3:45 p.m.

"Oddly, the crowd, which totalled 34,072, was larger than either of the gatherings that turned out for the two weekend games in Flatbush. The appearance of the additional few hundred in a sweltering arena doubtless was inspired by a desire to see whether the Dodgers could conceive of still one more way of losing a ball game.

"However, Leo Durocher's dashing Dodgers, apparently wearied of dashing their heads against an impenetrable wall, seemingly had run out of ideas. There was some snapping and snarling midway in the conflict, but in the closing rounds Brooklyn's so-called Beautiful Bums followed the pattern of almost all other National League champions whose luck has been to be paired against this flawless Yankee machine in a World Series.

"They quietly reconciled themselves to the futility of it all and retreated with as good grace as circumstances would permit. It was a sad spectacle for thousands of die-hards who suffered excruciatingly in the intense heat, but there was no help from it.

"Ernie Bonham, called 'Tiny' because he scales about 220 pounds, took the mound as McCarthy's fifth starting pitcher in the series, and by throttling the Brooklyn attack down to four meager hits, matched Marius Russo's stellar performance last Saturday. Like Russo, he won his first World Series game. . . .

"Thus, for the ninth time in the twelve World Series they have appeared in since 1921, the Yankees have stalked off with the winner's share of the spoils. McCarthy has led them to six of these triumphs in the last ten seasons. He now has won more world titles [six] than any other manager. . . .

"Tearing the league apart in midsummer, [the Yanks] clinched their flag on Sept. 4, the earliest in the history of their circuit, and by the record margin of 20 games."

Chapter 13
27th thru 30th: Yanks Twice, Reds and Red Sox

27. 1938 Yankees

Members of Hall of Fame: 4.

The Yanks had the same team that had won the pennant the previous two years except for two new starters: Joe Gordon at second base and Tommy Henrich in right field.

Among all pennant winners, the club tied for first in World Series Net and placed eighth in Runs.

Joe DiMaggio batted .324 and had 140 runs batted in. He had 32 home runs. Bill Dickey batted .313 with 115 RBI and 27 homers. Red Rolfe batted .311. Lou Gehrig had 114 runs batted in and 29 home runs. It was his last full season.

Red Ruffing led the pitchers with a league leading 21 wins against 7 losses. Lefty Gomez was 18—12 and Monte Pearson was 16—7.

John Drebinger of the *New York Times* on Oct. 3, 1938, previewed the upcoming World Series between the Yankees and the Chicago Cubs:

"In this coming meeting, we have on the one side the Yanks, a superbly balanced club that functions almost to perfection when the chips are down, pitted against an array which, analyzed coldly, seems to have nothing very prepossessing about it, yet has done some remarkable things. It is a club which, motivated by that intangible something called inspirational play, got so insufferably hot in a torrid pennant race it literally seared its way to the top. . . .

"Off the records, one must say the Yankees should win this series swiftly, decisively and hands down. They have achieved the same smashing success as the great Yankee teams of previous years and have accomplished it with an even greater display of team play than any of their predecessors. Perhaps never in all baseball history has a ball club functioned so efficiently as a unit as these Yankees of 1938.

"This is clearly revealed in the records. For, with the exception of Charlie Ruffing's fine pitching mark, none of the season's individual major honors will fall to any of the Yanks.

"Yet, as a whole, the team performs with amazing efficiency. No fewer than four clubs in the American League outrank the Yankees in team batting averages. Still, in the all-important runs batted in column as well as in home runs, the McCarthymen far excel all their rivals in their own league as well as anything the National League has to offer.

"Even more striking is the even distribution of this power. Although their leading home run clouter, Joe DiMaggio, has hit 32, the Yanks have no fewer than five men who have hit more than 20! . . .

"Henrich and Gordon together have compiled nearly 50 homers and driven in a total of just short of 200 tallies. . . .

"It is to this even distribution of strength and the devastating power behind their long-range shots that the Yanks owe their success. That, and the uniformly commendable pitching they receive from Ruffing, Lefty

Gomez, Monte Pearson, Bump Hadley and the youthful Spud Chandler, along with the excellent relief work of Johnny Murphy.

"DiMaggio, Bill Dickey and Lou Gehrig are still their mightiest siege guns. But from the top, where you find Frankie Crosetti and Red Rolfe, down to the bottom, where lurk George Selkirk and Gordon, you have an over-powering battlefront capable of rendering any pitcher apart at any given moment.

"It is a combination that for three years has established itself as absolutely invincible and one that must be considered as such until actually toppled.

"But, cool analysis means nothing to a team as hot as the Cubs have been these last three weeks."

Two days later, *Times* sports columnist John Kieran gave his assessment of the series ahead:

"Frankly, and most baseball fans will agree, the Yankees look like the stronger club. Marse Joe McCarthy thinks it's the best club baseball ever saw and Connie Mack was quoted as agreeing with that unprejudiced verdict. . . .

"There is the further point urged by some serious thinkers that a third straight world championship in baseball is too much to expect of any club. It never has happened yet. Somehow, that doesn't seem a very convincing argument. There must always be a first time for everything."

The Yankees went on to do the "unexpected." John Drebinger reported on the series result in the Oct. 10 *Times*:

"Baseball history was made yesterday as the Yankees again conquered the Cubs, 8 to 3, and captured the 1938 World Series by four games to none.

"The triumph gave the New Yorkers the distinction of being the first club ever to annex three successive world championships. . . .

"The final battle at the Stadium yesterday, viewed by 59,847 onlookers seemed merely a repetition of what had gone before, only there was more emphasis to it.

"Burly Red Ruffing, victor in the series opener in Chicago last Wednesday, came back to spin another commendable performance on the mound, and behind him there again was the steady drumfire of long-range blows that tossed the Cubs into hopeless confusion whenever they made the slightest mistake. Perhaps their greatest mistake was in showing up at all. . . .

"[Cub Manager Gabby Hartnett] hurled no fewer than six pitchers into the futile struggle, which in itself constitutes another World Series record. Gabby started with Bill Lee, victim of the first game. . . .

"Then came an almost endless procession of hurlers, the veteran Charlie Root, the rookie Vance Page, the left-handed Larry French, Tex Carleton and finally, with a gesture more theatrical than effective, the great man [Dizzy] Dean himself. . . .

"It was . . . the fourth time the Yanks had recorded a grand slam of four straight. They first achieved this feat in 1927 at the expense of the [Pittsburgh] Pirates, repeated the stunt with the [St. Louis] Cardinals in 1928, and in 1932, their next World Series appearance, bowled over the Cubs without losing a game. . . .

"All told, over a span of 12 campaigns, this astounding New York club has brought to the American League six world championships by winning 24 games and losing only 3."

John Kieran's column in the *Times* the same day reflected his view that the Yankees were far better than their series opponent:

"Anyway, the Cubs saved their lives. Rather painfully for the club owners, baseball once again proved that it is honest. If the Cubs had won a game from the

Yankees, there might have been loud cries of 'fake!' and demand for a federal inquiry."

John Drebinger commented further in the Oct. 11 *Times* on the gap between the Yanks and the National League representative:

"The pronounced superiority of the Yanks over their National League rivals deprived this series of all semblance of exciting competition. The one dramatic moment came in that memorable second game when Dizzy Dean, the celebrated hollow shell, made his heroic bid to stem the tide. The audacity of the fellow in trying to check that juggernaut with nothing more than craft and cunning will not be forgotten.

"But . . . his efforts went to waste. The Yanks had first class, commendable pitching every step, and behind that they had eight highly skilled and talented performers. . . .

"And so another off-season rolls around with the dominant question, 'What's to be done about those Yanks?'

"Very likely, not a great deal. By an amazing system of organization the Yanks have built themselves into their present great structure under conditions wholly permissible, and there is little the seven remaining battered clubs in the American League or the routed National League pennant victors can do about the matter."

28. 1975 Reds

Members of Hall of Fame: 2.

The Reds coasted to an easy win in the National League's West division, winning by 20 games (third best in the Games Ahead of Second category). They went on to beat Pittsburgh three straight in the league playoffs.

Five foot, seven inch second baseman Joe Morgan,

who had been obtained from Houston, batted .327 for the "Big Red Machine." He was one of the Red team leaders.

Pete Rose, at third base, batted .317. Right fielder Ken Griffey hit .305. Left fielder George Foster batted .300 with 23 home runs.

Catcher Johnny Bench, who had been drafted by the Reds in 1965 as a pitcher, hit 28 homers and had 110 RBI. As a catcher, Bench won ten straight Golden Glove awards and by the time of his retirement, hit more home runs than any other catcher in major league history.

First baseman Tony Perez hit 20 homers and had 109 RBI. Pitcher Don Gullett was 15 and 4. The Reds had two great freshman relievers, Rawly Eastwick, who had a league leading 22 saves, and Will McEnaney, who had 15.

During the first six weeks of the season, the Reds lost more games than they won. Then, Manager Sparky Anderson moved Pete Rose from left field to third and the Reds won 90 of their last 125 games to establish their final 20-game division advantage.

The upcoming league playoff with the Pittsburgh Pirates was discussed in the Oct. 4, 1975, *New York Times*:

"The Reds . . . figure their advantage lies in base running and fielding. . . .

"[The Reds] stole 168 bases to the Pirates 49."

Dave Anderson, sports columnist for the *Times*, commented on the playoff opener the next day:

"Today, Don Gullett, Joe Morgan and Ken Griffey . . . justified the vibrations of this great baseball city on the Ohio River. . . .

"Gullett, a 24-year old left hander with a polite manner and an impolite fast ball, scattered eight hits, fielded his position like a mongoose and hit a home run - his first since he used to play in the Kentucky hills."

The Reds won that first game 8-3 and swept the series three games to none.

Murray Chass gave his view of the World Series to follow with the Boston Red Sox in the Oct. 10 *Times*:

"The Cincinnati Reds figure to flood Fenway Park with a torrent of home runs. . . .

"[They] figure to run the Boston Red Sox dizzy with their base stealing tactics. . . .

"[They] figure to outplay the Red Sox because of their postseason experience. . . .

"On paper and past history, the Reds appear to possess the stronger team, but no team . . . ever won any series on paper or past performance. . . .

"There's little doubt the Reds have a wealthier collection of talented players than the Red Sox - Joe Morgan, Pete Rose, Johnny Bench, Tony Perez and Dave Concepcion for starters. . . .

"The Red Sox won the American League playoffs because their starting pitchers pitched better than expected, their relief pitchers relieved better than expected and Carl Yastrzemski played better than expected.

"Whether this same combination, or variations, will overcome the Reds remains to be seen.

"In winning 108 games during the regular season, the Reds had four .300 hitters in their line-up and five players who drove in 74 runs or more.

"It might seem likely that players such as Bench, Perez and George Foster, who hit 71 home runs among them, will clear the Green Monster of a left field wall easily. . . .

"The Reds are favored to win because of the solid nature of their lineup and their bullpen."

Dave Anderson described the exciting World Series that ended finally with a Reds' victory in the seventh and deciding game in the *Times* on Oct. 23:

"BOSTON. OCT. 22. It ended the way it had to, this World Series that the Cincinnati Reds won but that the Boston Red Sox didn't lose; the Red Sox just didn't win. If baseball games went ten innings instead of nine, perhaps the Red Sox would have won. But time ran out on them when Carl Yastrzemski lifted a high fly to center field tonight. . . .

"The drama in seven acts had ended at the Fenway theater with the Reds winning, 4-3, the score of the game and the score of the World Series that reminded the nation how beautiful baseball can be when it means something. To the Reds, who had lost the World Series in both 1972 and 1970, it meant everything, especially to Pete Rose, who figured in all three of the Reds' scoring innings after the Red Sox had taken a 3-0 lead in the third. . . .

"He . . . has an American Motors automobile as the most valuable player in this series, courtesy of *Sport* magazine. He earned it with four contributions in a crisis - three as a batter, one as a third baseman. . . .

"The real winner of this World Series was baseball itself. . . .

"When a baseball game means something, as it does in a World Series or the league playoffs or in a pennant race, baseball is the best game. . . . In the hours before tonight's decisive game, the more excitable critics were calling the sixth game 'the greatest' in baseball history. The more restrained observers were describing it as 'one of the best,' which indeed it was as the Red Sox won 7-6 on Carlton Fisk's homer off the left field foul pole in the 12th inning. But, tonight the Reds had their most memorable game.

"More than anything else, this World Series was a reminder that baseball, when it means something, is the greatest game."

Joseph Durso used the *Times'* front page the same day to describe the final game:

"BOSTON. OCT. 22. In the final inning of the final game the Cincinnati Reds finally subdued the rambunctious Boston Red Sox, 4-3, tonight and won the 72nd World Series in seven games. . . .

"The big bad 'mean machine' of Cincinnati had captured the Reds' first championship in 35 years.

"It was the end of a series filled with new heroes, new geography and even new rivals. . . .

"'It was the greatest World Series ever played,' said Sparky Anderson, the white-haired 41-year-old manager of the Reds, who won 108 games in the National League this summer. 'I think we're the best team in baseball - but not by much.' . . .

"'I said last night's game was the best game ever played in baseball,' [Pete Rose added]. 'Now I take it back. This one's got to be the greatest.' . . .

"The Reds, with the best record in baseball, had managed to win 26 games in their final turn at bat this year and they were about to do their thing one more time. . . .

"Finally, with two down, Morgan, a left-handed batter, lobbed a single to short center field [to bring in the winning run]. . . .

"The series was the fourth in the last five years that went the full distance of seven games. . . . It proved to be as close as a series can get."

Columnist Red Smith also wrote about this great series. His report appeared in the Oct. 24 *Times*:

"The World Series was wonderful and hard on the nerves like a gifted entertainer who doesn't know how to get off stage. . . .

"Every schoolboy knows that Cincinnati is the birthplace of professional baseball. . . . Those Cincinnati Red

Stockings of 1869 were the world's first team of mercenaries, yet the championship won by Pete Rose and his accomplices after all these years was only the third ever brought to Cincinnati. . . .

"It is altogether possible that the Reds have been the best team in baseball for five years. . . .

"Nowhere can you find averages proving the simple truth that Johnny Bench is the finest ballplayer now in the game and Bench, Rose and Joe Morgan almost surely the most accomplished trio under contract to any single employer. . . .

"The 72nd World Series was a highly entertaining show. Probably, some will rank it best of all."

29. 1903 Pilgrims (later the Red Sox)

Members of Hall of Fame: 2.

Boston represented the three-year-old American League in the first World Series against the champ of the 28-year-old National League, the Pittsburgh Pirates.

Left fielder Patsy Dougherty batted .331. Buck Freeman, the right fielder, led the league in homers with 13 and in RBI with 104.

The great Cy Young, then 36 years old, led in pitching with a league-leading 28 wins against 9 losses. The team had three 20-game winners. Bill Dinneen was 21 and 13 and Long Tom Hughes was 20 and 7.

The crowd may have been small by modern standards, but the series outcome was still important to those in the stands. This report on the final game appeared in the sports pages of the *New York Times* on Oct. 14, 1903:

"BOSTON. OCT. 13. The Boston Americans shut out the Pittsburgh Nationals today and won the baseball world's championship to the almost frenzied delight of 7,000 enthusiasts. . . . The demonstration which followed Dinneen's striking out of Hans Wagner in the ninth equalled any college football game.

"[Deacon] Philippi, who was such an enigma to the Bostons in the first two games, assayed to pitch for the visitors for the sixth time. He was not only battered hard, but he saw his rival, Dinneen, carry off the honors by holding the Nationals down to four scattered hits, which backed by perfect fielding, prevented a single Pittsburgh man from getting further than third base. Dinneen struck out seven men and his support by [Boston catcher Lou] Criger contributed materially to the success of the game. . . .

"Boston's score would have undoubtedly been larger but for the great running catches of Beaumont and Clarke, Wagner's work at short and Leach's at third base. For the home team, [shortstop Freddy] Parent's hauling down of a liner from Clarke's bat roused the greatest enthusiasm."

The Pilgrims captured the series five games to three from the Pirates.

29. 1953 Yankees

Members of Hall of Fame: 3.

Manager Casey Stengel's Yankees easily won an unprecedented fifth straight American League pennant.

Gene Woodling in left batted .306. Hank Bauer in right batted .304. Yogi Berra, the catcher, had 27 homers and 108 RBI. Mickey Mantle in center had 21 homers and 92 runs batted in.

Young Whitey Ford, back after two years of military service, was 18—6. Johnny Sain was 14—7. Ed Lopat was 16—4 with a league leading 2.42 ERA. Allie Reynolds was 13—7.

To see what was being written about the Yankees and the Brooklyn Dodgers before they met in the World Series, check the reports under the 1953 Dodgers, the 21st best team.

John Drebinger wrapped up this "subway" series in the sports pages of the *New York Times* on Oct. 6, 1953:

"In a whirlwind, breathtaking finish that doubtless will be remembered as long as baseball is played, Casey Stengel's Yankees yesterday became the first team in history to win five World Series championships in a row. . . .

"A crowd of 62,370 roaring fans . . . saw the American League's amazing Bombers vanquish a fighting band of Dodgers, 4 to 3, to clinch the 1953 classic by a margin of 4 games to 2. . . .

"In the last half of the ninth, amazing Bill Martin, doubtless cast from the start to fill the hero's role, slammed a single into center field off relief hurler Clem Labine. That shot, which gave Billy a series record of 12 hits, sent Hank Bauer racing over the plate with the decisive tally.

"And so, to 63-year-old Charles Dillon Stengel, who in some 40 odd years has just about touched all the bases in an astounding career, now goes the distinction of becoming the first manager to match five straight pennants with five straight world's titles.

"He did it, too, in his first five years in the American League, for prior to 1949 the 'Ol' Perfessor,' as the gravel voiced philosopher, sage and wit of the diamond is fondly known, had never so much as played, coached or managed a single inning in the junior circuit. . . .

"This was the seventh time that a Dodger team had tried and failed to [win] its first World Series crown."

Arthur Daley added his view in a *Times* column Oct. 7:

"The Bronx Bombers always take with them into crucial combat a psychological factor that's of inestimable advantage. The tradition of invincibility is a potent weapon. . . .

"A couple of seasons ago at spring training, Charles Dillon Stengel stated flatly that his Yankees would win the pennant again.

"'Do you mean to claim that the Yanks have the best team?' asked this listener, a note of incredulity in his voice.

"'That ain't got nothin' to do with it,' growled the Ol' Perfessor. 'I didn't say we had the best team. I just said we'd win.' . . .

"The Yanks didn't necessarily have the better team in the World Series, either. But they won. . . .

"It's impossible to overlook the fact that the Yankees were opportunists supreme. . . .

"The second big factor was Stengel. There's no getting away from it. The Ol' Perfessor is psychic. As far as strategy is concerned, he has the Midas touch."

Chapter 14
Top 20 Teams Since World War II

Only six post-World War II teams made the Top 30. As there have been 96 pennant winners since the war, this means that only 6% of them made our select list. As can be seen in Table 15, more than one-third (34%) of the pre-World War I teams made the Top 30 and 20% of the pennant winners between the two great wars made it.

The Top 30 teams that played before World War II are compared in Table 16 with those that played after that war.

Table 15
The Top 30 by Time Period

Time Period	Number of Pennant Winners	Number in Top 30	%
1901-1916	32	11	34
1917-1918	4	0	-
1919-1941	46	9	20
1942-1945	8	4	50
1946-1993	96	6	6
TOTAL	186	30	16%

It is hard to understand why so many pennant winners who played before World War I made the Top 30 when modern baseball was just getting started, while so few post-WWII teams made it.

It can be argued that the decline of the minor leagues

following World War II and the expansion of the number of Big League teams starting in 1961 resulted in a dilution of talent available for any one team, but there is no mathematical way to adjust for these considerations. Further discussion of this situation will appear later.

Best 20 Baseball Teams Since World War II

As reported earlier, the 1969 Baltimore Orioles were the best team since World War II; the 1954 Cleveland Indians were the second best; the 1953 Brooklyn Dodgers, the third best; the 1986 New York Mets, fourth; the 1975 Cincinnati Reds, fifth; and the 1953 New York Yankees, sixth best.

In Table 16, we show the 20 best teams since World War II, adding 14 to the six that made the Top 30.

Table 16
The 20 Best Teams Since World War II and
their composite scores

1. 1969 Baltimore Orioles 79.8
2. 1954 Cleveland Indians 78.6
3. 1953 Brooklyn Dodgers 76.0
4. 1986 New York Mets 74.6
5. 1975 Cincinnati Reds 73.3
6. 1953 New York Yankees 73.0
7. 1948 Cleveland Indians 68.9
8. 1970 Baltimore Orioles 68.6
9. 1961 New York Yankees 68.1
10. 1984 Detroit Tigers 63.7
11. 1955 Brooklyn Dodgers 63.4
12. 1957 New York Yankees 61.6
12. 1958 New York Yankees 61.6
14. 1956 New York Yankees 61.4
15. 1954 New York Giants 61.2
16. 1946 Boston Red Sox 60.0

In the following pages, we take a closer look at the 14 of these postwar teams which have not already been covered.

Chapter 15
A Closer Look at the Rest of the Best Postwar Teams

7. 1948 Indians

Members of Hall of Fame: 4.

The 1948 Cleveland Indians had the second best team pitching in history. They were second in Net Earned Run Average with 1.06 better than the American League average in 1948. They also were a slugging team, ranking 11th among all pennant winners in Net Slugging Average and 11th in Net Home Runs.

Rookie pitcher Gene Bearden led the league in ERA with 2.43. He had a 20—7 record. Bob Lemon was also a 20-game winner, with a 20-14 record and a 2.82 ERA. Bob Feller won 19 games and lost 15 with an ERA of 3.56. Russ Christopher was their leading reliever, with 17 saves and a 2.90 ERA.

But, one of the most exciting pitchers on the team was Satchel Paige, the legendary black hurler, hired by owner Bill Veeck at the age of 41 to shore up the pitching staff. Paige won 6 and lost 1 and had an ERA of 2.47.

Player-Manager Lou Boudreau, the shortstop, led the team in batting with .355, 106 RBI and 18 home runs. Right fielder Larry Doby, the first black player in the American League, who had joined the Indians the previous season, batted .301.

Second baseman Joe Gordon led the team in homers and RBI with 32 and 124 respectively. Left fielder Dale Mitchell batted .336. Third baseman Ken Keltner had 31 home runs and 119 RBI.

Boudreau almost single-handedly won the pennant for the Indians in a one-game postseason playoff with the Boston Red Sox. John Drebinger described the Indian victory on page 1 of the Oct. 5, 1948, *New York Times*:

"BOSTON. OCT. 4. Cleveland is to have its first World Series in 28 years.

"This became an actuality today as the Indians, fired by the inspirational leadership of their talented skipper, Lou Boudreau, crushed Joe McCarthy's Red Sox in the single game that had been found necessary to break the deadlock in the American League 1948 scramble.

"The playoff, first in the history of the junior circuit, was witnessed by a crowd of 33,957 shivering fans, most of whom watched it in glum silence. It was decided by an 8-to-3 score, and as a consequence, the Indians will oppose the National League champion Braves when the World Series opens here Wednesday.

"It marked only the second American League flag to be won by Cleveland and the first since 1920, when Tris Speaker, the famed Grey Eagle, led another band of Indians to a pennant as well as a subsequent world championship.

"There never was much doubt of the outcome on this crisp autumnal afternoon. For the Tribe, which in the last few days of one of the most thrilling pennant races in major league history, had flubbed a couple of chances to win the flag outright over the regular 154-game schedule, this time shot straight for the mark.

"Behind the stout-hearted five-hit hurling of Gene Bearden, 27-year-old southpaw freshman, . . . Manager

Boudreau blazed the trail with two home runs. Ken Keltner blasted another with two comrades aboard to spark a bruising four-run fourth inning, and that about tells the story.

"Boudreau's play throughout was truly phenomenal. The personable graduate of the University of Illinois who in 1942 at the age of 25 became the youngest manager ever to direct a major league club, gave a performance seldom matched by any player in a struggle of such vast importance.

"Playing his own position at shortstop flawlessly, maneuvering his men hither and yon with rare judgment and watching like a hawk every pitch of his youthful moundsman, Lou still found time not only to larrup two homers over the left field barrier, but added two singles, each of which figured in further scores.

"Against this demonstration, Joe McCarthy, completing his first year as manager of the Red Sox, and winner of eight American League pennants as field general of the Yankees, suddenly found himself completely out of ammunition."

Arthur Daley also commented on the playoff result in his column the same day in the *Times*:

"Lou Boudreau, who probably doesn't know any better, risked everything on his stylish young southpaw, Gene Bearden. Fenway Park is supposed to be poison on left-handed pitchers, particularly when the wind blows the wrong way. But Bearden fed the poison in large doses to the Red Sox and killed their pennant chances. . . .

"The story of this first playoff in the history of the American League is the story of the busy bees - or the Busy B's, Bearden and Boudreau. . . .

"Manager Boudreau had one big advantage over Manager McCarthy. He had player Boudreau performing for him and that's worth more than all the mental gymnastics from here to St. Louis and back. Not only did Lou play shortstop as though he'd invented the job, but he was a rather handy guy with a bat. . . .

"It merely was a four-for-four job on the most important day of his entire career. The Indians made eight runs. Boudreau had a hand in the manufacture of six of them. The man is slow. He's held together by adhesive tape. His batting form is atrocious. But what a ballplayer he is!"

John Drebinger previewed the World Series in the Oct. 6 *Times*:

"The betting gentry, in fact, already have indicated clearly which way the wind is expected to blow. . . . The Indians are quoted favorites to win the series at 5 to 12. . . .

"Regarding the remainder of his battlefront, Boudreau, noted for startling innovations and spectacular playing manipulations that at times have rivaled those of Leo Durocher, . . . indicated that he planned to go along extremely conservative lines. The only shifts he contemplates will be in right field. . . .

"Ed Robinson will go all the way at first for the Tribe and in center field will be Larry Doby, Negro star who becomes the second member of his race to appear as a regular in the classic. Brooklyn's Jackie Robinson was the first last October. . . .

"The vast majority of observers seem to feel that the Indians, despite the terrific battle they had in their own league from the Red Sox, Yankees and Athletics, have too much overall strength and so-called 'class' for their rivals.

"This seems to reveal itself everywhere except perhaps in the outfield. In pitching, the Clevelanders are coming to the mark with three formidable starting hurlers in Feller, Lemon and Bearden, backed up by two highly capable and reliable relief operatives in Russ Christopher and the veteran Negro star, Paige.

"Their infield, sparked by the super-brilliant Boudreau at short, the spectacular if at times erratic Joe Gordon at second and the hard-clouting Ken Keltner at third, ranks among the best in the game today. Behind the plate, the Tribe likewise rates among the top with Jim Hegan, who will catch all the games."

The Indians went on to take the series in six games. John Drebinger reported on the final game on the front page of the Oct. 12 *Times*:

"BOSTON. OCT. 11. Under a leaden sky that threatened any moment to shed bitter tears on the scene, Lou Boudreau and his Indians today crowned themselves baseball champions of the universe by defeating the Braves in the sixth game of the 1948 World Series. . . .

"The Tribe played grim, tight-lipped ball, made few mistakes and came home in front, 4 to 3.

"That gave the Indians the series, four games to two, and placed Boudreau's cast alongside Tris Speaker's immortals who in 1920 triumphed in the only other fall classic in which Cleveland has appeared. . . .

"The victory . . . gave the American League its 28th triumph against 17 for the National circuit. . . .

"Locked in a one-all mound duel, Joe Gordon, the sterling second sacker . . . slammed a homer in the sixth inning and with that shot the tide of battle remained with the Indians. . . .

"Today, as so many times previously this season, the resourceful Boudreau showed that his players still had the 'winning class' when the chips were down and few will deny that their final triumph was well merited."

Arthur Daley's column in the Oct. 12 *Times* also looked at the series just finished:

"A silly sport, baseball. Bob Lemon pitches two very indifferent ball games and emerges as the only double winner of the series. And the great Bob Feller loses two. You may figure that one out at your leisure. You will have until April to do your figuring."

8. 1970 Orioles

Members of Hall of Fame: 3.

The 1970 Orioles were ranked third, fourth, ninth, and 16th best in other studies of the greatest teams ever.

This team was made up of almost the same players as the 1969 Oriole team which ranked 12th among all teams in this study and was the best since World War II.

Boog Powell, first baseman, led the team in hitting with 35 home runs, 114 RBI and a batting average of .297. Right fielder Frank Robinson led the team in batting average with .306 and had 25 homers and 78 RBI.

The team also had two infielders renowned for their brilliant fielding in third baseman Brooks Robinson and shortstop Mark Belanger.

But, the team's greatest strength was its pitching, featuring three 20-game winners. Mike Cuellar and Dave McNally tied for the league lead in wins with 24. Cuellar's record was 24-8, with an ERA of 3.47 and McNally was 24-9 and 3.22. Jim Palmer won 20 and lost 10 with a 2.71 ERA.

Leonard Koppett of the *New York Times* reported Oct. 6, 1970 on the Orioles' league championship series against the Minnesota Twins:

"For the second straight year, the Baltimore Orioles brushed aside the Minnesota Twins for the third straight game to win the championship of the split American League. Today's score was 6-1 with Jim

Palmer pitching a seven-hitter in which he struck out 12 men.

"The Orioles have won three of the last five American League pennants and have a respectable dynasty going."

Murray Chass previewed the upcoming World Series against Cincinnati in the *Times* two days later:

"Jim Palmer, Mike Cuellar and Dave McNally will try to do to the Cincinnati Reds this year what they couldn't do to the New York Mets last year - beat them in the World Series.

"The Baltimore pitchers had been expected to handle the Mets without too much trouble, but Tom Seaver, Jerry Koosman and Gary Gentry - with an assist from New York's hitters and fielders - foiled their plans. . . .

"The Reds, empirical evidence shows, offer a more potent run producing threat to Baltimore than the Mets did, but on a pitching basis the Orioles clearly come out ahead.

"Earl Weaver, the impish Baltimore manager who has mentally replayed the 1969 series throughout 1970, named his pitching rotation yesterday, selecting Palmer to open Saturday against [Gary] Nolan. Cuellar will pitch the second game and McNally the third. . . .

"Palmer is low man on Baltimore's 20-game winner pole. . . . Nevertheless, he is likely the best pitcher on the team and he also is a right hander.

"Weaver especially took the latter point into consideration in selecting the 24-year-old fast baller to start and then pitch the fourth game and the seventh, if necessary. The Reds won three- fourths of the games left handers started against them, . . . and Cuellar and McNally are left handers.

"On the other hand, there's one difference between Cuellar and most other southpaws. The 33-year-old Cuban throws a screwball, which makes him more effective than other lefties against right- handed hitters."

Chass added this in the Oct. 9 *Times*:

"The Orioles scored more runs than the Reds during the season, 792 to 775, but the Reds hit more homers, 191 to 179, and had a significantly better team batting average, .270 to .257. . . .

"Defensively, the teams are evenly matched in the outfield; Bench is well ahead of Andy Etchebarren and Elrod Hendricks, the Baltimore catchers; and each team has a standout player in the infield.

"The Orioles' infield gem is Brooks Robinson, the third baseman, who always seems to come up with great plays in important games."

Joseph Durso reported on the Orioles' five-game World Series triumph in the *Times* on Oct. 16:

"BALTIMORE. OCT. 15. One year after their memorable loss to the New York Mets, the Baltimore Orioles batted their way to a 9-3 victory over the Cincinnati Reds today and captured the 67th World Series, four games to one.

"Spotting the National League champions three runs in the first inning, they charged back with six of their own inside three innings. And by the time Brooks Robinson threw out the last Cincinnati batter to end the game, they had pounded six pitchers for 15 hits and convincingly won the championship of baseball.

"It was an awesome display by a team that was upset in five games by the Mets last October and every man in the lineup contributed to it. All eight regulars got hits, including home runs by Frank Robinson and Merv Rettenmund, and the only Oriole who did not get a hit was Mike Cuellar, the pitcher.

"But Cuellar . . . lent a hand with the fanciest pitching of the series. Troubled by a bad hip and rattled by the three-run burst at the start, he allowed Cincinnati only two singles and a walk over the last eight innings and retired 23 of the final 26 batters.

"For the Orioles, who dominated the American League for the last two years, the victory marked them as the closest thing to a dynasty in baseball - a sport that has become the graveyard for 'dynasties' in recent years.

"They have played in three World Series in five years, have taken two of them and have won two of every three games during the last two seasons."

Times sports columnist Arthur Daley also commented the same day on the Orioles' success:

"Resplendent in the murky half light of a miserable day, the Baltimores completed the dismantlement of the Big Red Machine and became champions of the world. . . .

"The Orioles thus have succeeded the Mets as champions of the world. They did it by using the Met formula of getting all the breaks and making with the magic. This time it was Brooks Robinson as the chief magician instead of Tommie Agee, Ron Swoboda & Co. It produced the same result, too, four of five in victories.

"And as one final flourish, one last dazzling forget-me-not, Brooksie made another fantastic catch of a bullet drive by John Bench for the first out in the ninth. It symbolized Baltimore's preeminence."

Leonard Koppett added his view the next day in the *Times*:

"Even while the champagne was still squirting after Baltimore's decisive victory over Cincinnati in the World Series Thursday, players of both teams and any number of their fans were conceding the 1971 pennants to each other, promising a rematch in next fall's World Series.

"In fact, admirers of the Orioles and Reds set a World Series record: most dynasties born, one series - 2.

"It is usual enough for the winner of a World Series to be proclaimed the founder of a dynasty, especially if the victory is one-sided and the winning roster contains half a dozen players younger than 35. . . .

"But it is virtually unparalleled for the World Series loser, along with the winner, to be hailed as a dynasty. . . .

"These two teams were clearly the best in baseball in 1970. The Reds, especially, but the Orioles, too, are loaded with outstanding players still in their 20's. That they should have contending teams for years to come - as they have had for years past, for that matter - is a legitimate assumption.

"But being sure to win again is something else. . . .

"None of this detracts from the accomplishments of the Orioles and the Reds this season. They were, and will be, outstanding and attractive baseball teams. But making dates a year ahead is a risky business and all the forces of present day baseball structure work against the establishment by anyone of the sort of dynasties the Yankees, the Dodgers, the Cardinals, and longer ago, the Giants and Philadelphia Athletics, used to enjoy."

NOTE: In 1971, the Reds finished fourth in their division and the Orioles won the American League pennant but lost the World Series. In 1972, the Reds won the National League pennant but lost the World Series; the Orioles finished third in their division. In 1973, the Reds won their division but not the NL pennant; the Orioles won their division but not the AL pennant.

In 1974, the Reds were second in their division; the Orioles won their division but not the pennant. In 1975, the Reds won the World Series; the Orioles finished second in their division. In 1976, the Reds swept the World

Series; the Orioles were second in their division.

9. 1961 Yankees

Members of Hall of Fame: 3.

The 1961 Yanks were ranked the second best team of all time by one study and fifth by another. Two others ranked them sixth and another ranked them in the Top 10.

Roger Maris broke the single season home run record playing for this team, hammering 61. The right fielder also had 142 RBI.

Catcher Elston Howard batted .348. Mickey Mantle, the center fielder, batted .317, had 54 homers and 128 runs batted in.

Whitey Ford led the league in wins with 25 against only 4 losses. Ralph Terry was 16 and 3. Luis Arroyo led the league with 29 saves.

These Yankees placed fourth in Net Home Runs among the pennant winners.

The World Series against the Cincinnati Reds was previewed in an article on the sports pages of the Oct. 1, 1961 *New York Times*:

"One of the most intriguing World Series in recent years is due this week. . . .

"In one corner will be New York's perennial World Series entry, the Yankees. Under their new manager, Ralph Houk, they won their 26th American League pennant.

"In the other corner will be a rather unfamiliar but piquant group, the Cincinnati Reds.

"It has been 21 years since the Reds last made an appearance in baseball's autumn spectacle. . . .

"As for the forthcoming conflict, any number of baseball's outstanding academic minds haven't figured out yet how Freddie Hutchinson and his strange assortment of youngsters and castoffs ever managed to win the National League pennant.

"With extraordinary unanimity, virtually all the experts in the land dismissed the Cincinnatians last spring with the remark that they would be lucky to finish the season, let alone anywhere near the first division. . . .

"Under Houk's first-year leadership, the Yanks enter this World Series with an overwhelming array of talent. The stars include Roger Maris and Mickey Mantle, the home run wonders; the victory laden Whitey Ford; the young mound heroes, Bill Stafford and Roland Sheldon and the incomparable relief pitcher, Luis Arroyo."

Sports columnist Arthur Daley gave his view in the *Times* the next day:

"The baseball experts never learn. They start with strong opinions and then get wafted away by delusions of infallibility. It's a cinch, therefore, that they will talk themselves into picking the Yankees to crush the Cincinnati Reds in the forthcoming World Series. The longer they ponder the matter the more convinced they will become that this steamroller job will require the minimum of four games.

"Don't look now, but these are the same experts who selected the Redlegs to finish sixth in the National League pennant race. . . .

"But the amazing Zinzinnati Zingers have zipped off with the championship. . . .

"From a purely statistical standpoint the weight of evidence is on the side of the Yankees. Although the pitching is fairly even - this is an oversimplification - the coming series could very well be a hitters' series. And the Yanks have more and better hitters. . . .

"[The Yanks] have pounded more homers than any other team in baseball history. But Maris, Mantle and the clumsily adroit Berra form a fine outfield. Howard is supreme as a catcher. Boyer, Kubek and Richardson, three full-fledged magicians, perform feats of legerdemain in the infield. Supplementing them is Skowron, whose high competence as a first baseman is obscured by their collective brilliance. . . .

"It's the intangibles that make a guy wary. Caution has made this selector so cowardly that he picks the Yankees to win the World Series in five games."

On Oct. 3, John Drebinger of the *Times* also looked at the series ahead:

"This, to begin with, is not an attempt to predict the outcome of the World Series. Baseball's soothsayers know that even if the Yankees have won 18 of the 25 in which they have appeared, nothing can be more unpredictable than a World Series. . . .

"In defense, with its pitching and fielding, could lie the key to the outcome of the series.

"For on the attack, it must be conceded that the Cincinnatians are scarcely a match for the power laden Bombers. It is apparent that if [Manager] Freddie Hutchinson's Reds are to win they will have to rely heavily on defense.

"For let it not be overlooked that besides Roger Maris and Mickey Mantle, the Yanks have four other sluggers who have hit 20 or more homers this year.

"Have the Reds the pitchers to check this devastating hitting? . . .

"The staff may not be impressive in depth, but in the whirlwind brush of a World Series, depth is not too important. . . .

"Still, the Yanks seem to command a slight edge. Ralph Houk's staff not only is well balanced, but it has the advantage of experience.

"Whitey Ford, the Bombers' top money pitcher for

more than a decade, is a tremendous competitor. The southpaw has been through the mill and will be entering his eighth World Series.

"Though Whitey may tire in late innings, he never tires without giving ample warning. And that is where the amazing Luis Arroyo comes in. . . . He is one of the great relievers of modern times.

"Behind Ford are two accomplished youngsters, Bill Stafford and Ralph Terry. For the middle innings, there is also Roland Sheldon, the rookie star, Bud Daley, an artful knuckleballer, and Jim Coates. . . .

"Afield, the Yanks seem to have the edge. In the infield, the Bombers have four topflight performers. . . .

"No matter how Hutchinson shuffles, he cannot match the Yankee inner defense of Bill Skowron, Bobby Richardson, Tony Kubek and Cletis Boyer. . . .

"And behind the plate, Elston Howard, backed by John Blanchard and [Yogi] Berra, far overshadow the two Cincinnati rookies, John Edwards and Jerry Zimmerman, or Darrell Johnson, a former Yankee third string receiver. . . .

"The pick here has to be the Yankees in no more than five."

The Yankees did win in five. John Drebinger reported on the final game on the front page of the Oct. 10 *Times*:

"CINCINNATI. OCT. 9. The Yankees defeated the Cincinnati Reds today, 13 to 5, and won the World Series for the 19th time in 26 attempts.

"Eight Cincinnati pitchers gave a total of 15 hits, including home runs by John Blanchard and Hector Lopez. A five-run first inning started the Yankees to their fourth victory in the five games this series lasted."

Joseph M. Sheehan noted Manager Houk's series assessment in the *Times'* sports pages the same day:

"'They were all great! Everyone played his heart out.'

"Thus did Ralph Houk, a jubilant freshman manager who finished at the top of the baseball class, proudly hail his champion Yankees today after their series triumph over the Reds had been sealed with a booming barrage of base hits. . . .

"Houk praised the 1961 Bombers as the 'best all-around Yankee team' he had seen including the powerhouses of the early 1950s on which he had been a reserve catcher. . . .

"'This team has much more power down through the lineup and the finest defensive infield I ever have seen.'"

Sports columnist Arthur Daley commented further on the Yankee success in the *Times* of Oct. 11:

"It may well be that the Yankees had not won a more important World Series than the recently concluded horsehide festival in Cincinnati. Not in memory had American League prestige been so endangered or so vulnerable to ridicule as it was this time.

"The Nationals dominated interleague competition so completely in the last half-dozen years that they assumed the same condescending air of superiority that the Americans had been wearing since the days of Babe Ruth. They had the better ballplayers, the better league. That's what they claimed and they said it with such persistence that folks were beginning to believe them. . . .

"But the Nationals were so beautifully balanced and their strength was so awesomely distributed that even their sixth ranking team, the Cincinnati Reds, was able to win their championship. . . .

"The Yankees saved the American League from being disgraced.

"On what the Reds showed in this series, it would have been an utter disgrace, too. Every Cincinnati weakness surged to the surface and lay there nakedly. This was so bad a ball club that the genius of Freddie

Hutchinson shone forth. How did he ever contrive to win a pennant with so forlorn a band? Hutch had to be more than manager of the year. He had to be manager of the century. . . .

"This was a World Series that could be placed in the file-and- forget folder. It was dreary all the way, finishing on the ridiculous note of a 13-5 humiliation in the fifth and final game. The bright moments were few. . . .

"The future doesn't hold any rich promise for the National League, either. Expansion will dilute that loop for next year and the Yanks should be stronger because such kid pitchers as Ralph Terry, Bill Stafford and Roland Sheldon will be far more seasoned performers."

The Yanks won the American League pennant in each of the next three years but won the World Series only in 1962, beating the S.F. Giants four games to three.

10. 1984 Tigers

Members of Hall of Fame: 0.

The 1984 Tigers were ranked the 20th best team of all time in one study.

Alan Trammell, the shortstop, batted .314. Lance Parrish, the catcher, had 33 homers and Kirk Gibson, right fieldier, belted 27 more.

Jack Morris led the pitchers with a 19—11 record. Dan Petry was 18—8. Willie Hernandez had 32 saves.

On Oct. 2, 1984, Murray Chass of the *New York Times* previewed the American League championship playoff between the Tigers and the Kansas City Royals who would annex the World Title the next season:

"Never in the 16-year history of baseball's division playoff system has there been such a lopsided matchup as the American League has this week. If the Royals, who are host to Detroit in the first game, . . . had played in the same division as the Tigers, Kansas City would have finished 20 games behind. . . . .

But here they are, one step away from the World Series with an unspectacular record of 84 victories and 78 defeats, the worst ever for an American League playoff team. . . .

"[Detroit] won the American League East with a 104-58 record, best in the league since 1970. . . .

"The Tigers ran away with their division, winning 35 of their first 40 games and finishing with the best record in baseball. . . .

"The Tigers . . . are a collection of veteran players, many of whom have been together at Detroit for several years. The team did add some key players from other teams this year, and one of them, Willie Hernandez, the almost perfect relief pitcher, was highly instrumental in getting the Tigers to their first league championship series since 1972. . . .

"[Catcher] Lance Parrish is a vital member of the Tigers both offensively and defensively. . . . He led the team in home runs with 33 and runs batted in with 98.

"The heart of the infield . . . is the double play combination of Lou Whitaker at second and Alan Trammell at shortstop. No one has a better all-around infield. Trammell batted .314 and Whitaker .289. . . . .

"This was the season the Tigers have been expecting from Kirk Gibson for several years. The former collegiate football star batted .282, hit 27 homers and drove in 91 runs, finally shedding his platoon role for a full-time job. Chet Lemon, the center fielder, completes the best up-the-middle alignment in the majors, and this season batted .287 with 20 homers and 76 runs batted in. . . .

"Based on the season's performances, there should be no comparison between the two sets of starters. Jack

Morris was 19-11, Dan Petry 18-8 and Milt Wilcox 17-8 for the Tigers. Two of the Royals' four starters were under .500. . . .

"Morris won 10 of his first 11 decisions; Petry won 14 of his first 18 and Wilcox, his first six.

"Hernandez, whom the Tigers acquired from Philadelphia a week before the season started, had 32 saves and had not blown a save opportunity until last Friday night against the Yankees. . . .

"Hernandez, [who] throws a dandy screwball . . . can work often.

"[Manager] Anderson is in the playoffs for the sixth time, the first five having been with Cincinnati. The only time he lost was to the Mets in 1973. This year, he became the first manager in baseball history to win 100 games or more with two different franchises.

"A good bullpen is a trademark of an Anderson managed team, and the Tigers are no exception. No matter who his starter is or how good he is, Anderson will not hesitate to summon his relief corps. He wasn't named Captain Hook for nothing."

The Tigers swept the series with Kansas City 3 games to 0 to claim the pennant and advance to the World Series against the San Diego Padres.

The World Series was only slightly more competitive as the Tigers won it in five games. On Oct. 15, Chass reported in the *Times* on the final contest:

"DETROIT. OCT. 14. They led their division after their first game of the season, and now they lead the major leagues after their last.

"The Detroit Tigers, whose 104 regular season victories indicated that they were the best team in baseball this year, provided conclusive and irrefutable evidence today, winning the World Series with an 8-4 victory over the San Diego Padres.

"Climaxing a season in which they were in first place in the American League East every single day, the Tigers roared past the Padres, four games to one, by once again demolishing a San Diego starting pitcher in the early innings and adding a late inning touch of power.

"Kirk Gibson ... played the primary role in each instance by slugging two home runs halfway up the upper stands, and driving in five runs. . . .

"It took the Tigers only eight postseason games to become the champions. The last time anyone accomplished the feat in as few or fewer games was in 1976. . . .

"Sparky Anderson had become the only manager to win the World Series with teams in both leagues."

11. 1955 Dodgers

Members of Hall of Fame: 4.

This Dodger team was ranked among the best teams of all time by four other studies. They were ranked eighth best in two of the studies, 18th best in another and 21st best in still another.

The Dodgers were 98-55 and finished 13 1/2 games ahead of second.

They were led by center fielder Duke Snider who led the league with 136 RBI and batted .309 with 42 home runs. The catcher, Roy Campanella, batted .318 and hit 32 homers and had 107 RBI. Carl Furillo, the right fielder, batted .314, had 26 homers and 95 RBI. First baseman Gil Hodges had 27 homers and 102 RBI.

The intimidating Don Newcombe led the pitchers with a record of 20-5 and an ERA of 3.20. Clem Labine was 13-5 with 11 saves and an ERA of 3.24.

In the World Series, the Dodgers defeated the New York Yankees four games to three. This is almost the same team as the 1953 Dodgers, the 21st best team of all time.

12. 1957 Yankees

Members of Hall of Fame: 3.

Center fielder Mickey Mantle led the Yanks in batting, home runs and runs batted in. He batted .365, had 34 homers and 94 RBI.

Bill Skowron, the first baseman, batted .304. Catcher Yogi Berra had 24 homers.

Bobby Shantz led the American League in earned run average with 2.45. He won 11 and lost 5. Tom Sturdivant led the team in wins with a record of 16-6. He had a 2.54 ERA.

Bob Turley was 13-6 with a 2.71 ERA. Whitey Ford was 11-5 with a 2.57 ERA. Bob Grim led the team in saves with 19.

John Drebinger previewed the upcoming World Series against the Milwaukee Braves in the sports pages of the *New York Times* on Sept. 30, 1957:

"It is on the offense that a couple of Yankee casualties could be seriously felt for all the vaunted depth of Casey Stengel's reserves. For if neither Mickey Mantle nor Bill Skowron is able to play up to standard, the Yankee attack could be in trouble.

"A sound Mantle is the Bombers' key power hitter and since the Switcher clouts with equal force from either side of the plate, it matters little whether the opposition pitches a right hander or a southpaw. . . .

"There is, of course, ample power to be found throughout the Yankee battlefront. The game knows no more dangerous clutch hitter than Yogi Berra. . . .

"Gil McDougald hits both hard and often and the brilliant rookie, Tony Kubek, while not a home run slugger, hits often with drives that are deep and sharp. Also not to be overlooked is the venerable Enos Slaughter.

"'Old 41' was the spark that kept the Bombers going

last year after they had dropped the first two games at Ebbets Field. . . .

"Also ever dangerous are Hank Bauer and Elston Howard against left handers and Joe Collins and Harry Simpson against the right handers. . . .

"All in all, the advantage on the offense must be conceded to the Braves."

Drebinger compared the Yanks and Braves on defense the next day:

"A sound Mantle is just about as fine a center fielder as you will find in the majors. Perhaps not as flashy as a Willie Mays, but with his speed, capable enough of hauling down the toughest of shots in deep left center. . . .

"However, if the Switcher is unable to move around any faster than he did a few weeks ago, . . . the Yanks could again be in trouble.

"On the whole, though, the defensive edge does belong to the Yanks. . . .

"In pitching, which is the core of defensive play, the Yanks possess an amazingly well-balanced staff. They finished the season with five regular hurlers showing earned run averages of less than 3.00, an extraordinary record. This group consists of Whitey Ford, Bobby Shantz, Bob Grim, Tom Sturdivant and Bob Turley.

"Add to this quintet Don Larsen . . . plus Art Ditmar, Tommy Byrne, Johnny Kucks and Al Cicotte for relief, and you have a powerful staff. It explains why Stengel won his pennant so easily despite the fact that he did not have one pitcher close to being a 20-game winner. Sturdivant was tops with 15 victories. . . .

"At other defensive points . . . the Yanks do have a clear advantage. . . . Stengel has . . . a fine shortstop in Gil McDougald. . .

"Casey has two excellent third basemen in Andy Carey and Jerry Lumpe. One bats right handed, the other swings from the left. . .

"At short, Casey not only has McDougald but, along with his amazingly gifted rookie, Tony Kubek, who bats lefty, Casey boasts two of the most gifted performers to grace a single ball club. . .

"Comparing managerial tactics as well as managers, the advantage admittedly must go to the Bombers and this could well decide it. . . . Stengel . . . is in a class by himself. . . .

"It is Casey's resourcefulness, plus an extraordinary memory, that sets him apart from all present day managers. As a player and manager, Stengel has seen about everything that can happen on a ball field and has forgotten little of it. . . .

"As seen from this corner, the Yankees should win it, but only after a struggle that could go down to seven games."

Columnist Arthur Daley gave his view in the Oct. 2 *Times*:

"The Braves have the stronger and longer hitters. The Yanks have far greater speed and a far tighter defense. The defense may be extra important in this series, because both ball parks are roomy in the outfield. Those Braves outfielders are not the cleverest fly grabbers since DiMaggio. The best of them is Henry Aaron and he's a right fielder who has been drafted for center. . . .

"The choice here is the Braves in six games."

The Braves did win, but in seven games. John Drebinger filed a report after the final game for the *Times'* front page of Oct. 11:

"Milwaukee, which less than five years ago didn't even boast a major league club, bestrides the major league universe today.

"Manager Fred Haney's Braves playing inspired ball behind another brilliant pitching effort by their tireless Lew Burdette, smothered the supposedly invincible Yankees, 5 to 0, in the seventh and deciding World Series game at the Stadium yesterday.. . . .

"Burdette gained his third mound triumph of the classic [and] gave the National Leaguers the series four games to three. It brought to Milwaukee a world championship in its first crack at the title. . . .

"In little more than a month, Old Gotham had lost two ball clubs, the Dodgers and Giants. Yesterday, it was shorn of the World Series crown it had held, with one or another of its three entries, since 1949."

Arthur Daley provided his series wrap-up in the *Times* the same day:

"Burdette . . . pitched with exquisite artistry to gain his third victory and second shutout of the tournament.

"Burdette had the Bombers helpless."

12. 1958 Yankees

Members of Hall of Fame: 3.

The Yankees finished 92-62 and ten games ahead of the second- place Chicago White Sox.

Center fielder Mickey Mantle led the league in homers with 42. He batted .304 and knocked in 97 runs. Norm Siebern, in left, batted .300. Catcher Yogi Berra had 22 homers. Elston Howard, who played both outfield and catcher, batted .314.

Bob Turley led the league in wins. His record was 21-7. His ERA was 2.97. Whitey Ford led the league in ERA with 2.01. His record was 14-7. Ryne Duren had 20 saves and an ERA of 2.02.

The Yankees defeated the Milwaukee Braves four games to three in the World Series.

The team had many of the same players as the 1953

Yankees, the 29th best team of all time, and the 1961 Yankees, the eighth best team since World War II.

14. 1956 Yankees

Members of Hall of Fame: 4.

Center fielder Mickey Mantle led the Yankees. He won the baseball "Triple Crown" by leading the American League in batting with .353, in homers with 52 and in RBI with 130.

First baseman Bill Skowron batted .308 and hit 23 home runs. Shortstop Gil McDougald batted .311. Right fielder Hank Bauer had 26 home runs. Catcher Yogi Berra had 30 homers and 105 RBI.

Pitcher Whitey Ford notched the best mark for ERA in the league with 2.47, while winning 19 and losing 6.

Johnny Kucks was 18-9 with a 3.85 ERA. Tom Sturdivant was 16-8 with a 3.30 ERA. Don Larsen, who pitched the first perfect game in a World Series that year, was a respectable 11-5 with a 3.26 ERA.

John Drebinger previewed the series against the Brooklyn Dodgers in an article in the sports pages of the *New York Times* on Oct. 3, 1956:

"Buoying the hopes of the Bombers, who will be entering their 22nd World Series - they emerged victors in 16 - is the fact that in contrast to last fall, they are up to full strength.

"Spearheading their attack is Mickey Mantle who as the "Triple Crown" champion of the year . . . moves into this series as the dominant figure. Mickey the past season topped both major circuits with a .353 batting average, 52 homers and 130 runs batted in. Mantle, incidentally, becomes the first Triple Crown victor to engage in a World Series the same year. . . .

"Stengel's starting lineup offered virtually no surprises. He is leading off with Hank Bauer, followed by the 40-year-old Enos Slaughter who, on being picked up from the Athletics late in August has been staging quite a comeback of his own.

"Slaughter, who will patrol left field, is one of the few players to represent the two leagues in World Series play. He was with the Cards in 1942 when they tripped the Yankees and in 1946, it was his dash from first base on a double by Harry Walker that enabled the Redbirds to down the Red Sox.

"[Stengel's] infield will consist of Bill Skowron, Gil McDougald, both .300 hitters; Billy Martin, the hero of the 1953 series, and Andy Carey. The redoubtable Yogi Berra, who has played in every series for the Bombers since 1947, will again be behind the plate."

Arthur Daley looked at the series to come on Oct. 3 in the *Times*:

"'I gotta go with my professional,' Casey Stengel has been saying all along. He didn't identify his man, naturally enough. But he always refers to Whitey Ford as his professional. Come to think of it, there are normally only two types of ballplayers in the Stengel lexicon: 'professionals' and 'ribbon clerks.' . . .

"The main additions to the New York pitching staff have been young Johnny Kucks and young Tom Sturdivant. Both came from nowhere to save the situation for Ol' Case. . . .

"The choice here will be the Yankees, maybe in five games."

Don Larsen's perfect game in game five, only the fifth perfect game in Baseball's modern history, was the only one in series history. John Drebinger filed this report Oct. 9:

"Don Larsen is a footloose fellow of whom Casey Stengel once said, 'He can be one of baseball's great pitchers anytime he puts his mind to it.' Larsen had his mind on his work yesterday.

"He pitched the first no-hit game in World Series history. Not only that, but he also fired the first perfect game - no batter reaching first base - to be posted in the major leagues in 34 years.

"This nerve tingling performance, embellished with a Mickey Mantle home run, gained a 2-0 triumph for the Yankees over the Dodgers and Sal Maglie at the Stadium. It enabled Casey Stengel's Bombers to post their third straight victory for a 3-2 lead in the series. . . .

Drebinger later filed this report on the Yankees' seventh game championship victory:

"After a solid week of thrills, the 1956 World Series ended yesterday in an old and familiar pattern.

"The Yankees, whose virtual monopoly of the world championship had been interrupted last October, were back to reclaim their laurels in a welter of superlative performances.

"Casey Stengel's Bombers crushed the Dodgers in the seventh and deciding game at Ebbets Field, 9 to 0 . . . . It violently reversed last October's struggle when Walter Alston's Brooks bagged the seventh game to capture Brooklyn's first series title.

"Four home runs, the last a grand slam, fired behind the brilliant three-hit pitching of 23-year-old Johnny Kucks wrapped up this one. The amazing American League champions gained their 17th series title and sixth under the leadership of Charles Dillon Stengel."

15. 1954 Giants

Members of Hall of Fame: 3.

The 1954 New York Giants had outstanding pitching. They were the fourth best team in history in Net Earned Run Average, finishing .98 lower than the National League average.

The Giants were ranked the 15th best team of all time by another study.

The club also tied for first in World Series Net.

They were led by center fielder Willie Mays, arguably the best fielding center fielder of all time, who batted a league-leading .345, hit 41 home runs and batted in 110 runs.

Right fielder Don Mueller batted .342. Shortstop Alvin Dark hit 20 home runs. Third baseman Hank Thompson had 26 homers. Dusty Rhodes, a reserve outfielder, batted .341 and hit 15 home runs in only 164 at bats.

Pitcher Johnny Antonelli led the league in earned run average with 2.30. He won 21 and lost 7.

Ruben Gomez was 17—9 with an ERA of 2.88. Sal " The Barber" Maglie was 14-6 with a 3.26 ERA. Hoyt Wilhelm was 12-4 with an ERA of 2.10. Marv Grissom had 19 saves and an ERA of 2.35.

John Drebinger previewed the series between the Giants and the Cleveland Indians in the sports pages of the *New York Times* on Sept. 27, 1954. He discussed defense in this article:

"Baseball's academic minds . . . seem to agree on at least two counts. The 1954 World Series rivals certainly are the most evenly matched. And as a consequence, this could develop into a thrill- packed series in which one fielding slip, one badly pitched ball or one strategic mistake could be sufficient to decide the battle.

"Particularly is this true on the defense."

As noted earlier in the report on the 1954 Indians, the 16th best team of all time, Drebinger credited the Tribe with a pitching staff extraordinary in depth.

"Certain it is the Giants have no such depth to their staff," Drebinger commented. But, he pointed out that in a short series quantity is not as important as quality.

"And this the Polo Grounders do possess." He mentioned starters Antonelli, Maglie and Gomez and relievers Grissom and Wilhelm.

"Antonelli's pitching this year has been a revelation," Drebinger continued. "His 21-7 record just about wrapped up the pennant. Young and strong, Antonelli will have no difficulty starting twice and even three times if named for the opener and the series goes seven games.

"The 37-year-old Maglie made a grand comeback. He can't work as often as in former years, but the Barber still has days when he is as razor sharp as ever. He can go twice and win both times.

"At the other eight positions, the Giants must be given the upperhand defensively. Lockman at first base has a wide margin over Vic Wertz. . . .

"Davey Williams tops Bobby Avila [at second]. Davey in fact must be rated as one of the season's most underrated performers."

Drebinger added, "At short, Alvin Dark, while not flashy, is a tremendous competitor, invariably making the play that has to be made."

The sportswriter then described the Giants' outfield advantage. They had the "incomparable" Willie Mays "one of the great center fielders of our time."

He added that Wes Westrum of the Giants and the Indians' Jim Hegan were among the best catchers at the time.

Drebinger reported that both clubs had "high powered" offenses In another series preview the next day:

"The Giants can boast of having the National League's one, two batting punch [in Willie Mays and Don Mueller]. . . .

"Mays spearheads the Giant attack, but there is never any telling what Willie will do. He belts singles, doubles and triples most anywhere and while he didn't lead his league in homers, he did wind up with 41. . . .

"And behind Willie there is that deadly effective 'leg hitter,' Mueller, who, though he connected for only four homers, led both leagues in total hits with 212. Then there is Alvin Dark, one of the deadliest clutch hitters in the game, who hit 20 home runs, plus Henry Thompson, who smacked 26, and Whitey Lockman, who contributed 16 to the Giants' total of 186 homers as against 156 for the Tribe."

Drebinger concluded that the offensive advantage had to go to the Giants.

Columnist Arthur Daley also felt that the Giants' prospects were good, as reported earlier in the account of the 1954 Indians.

Despite being "contrary to logic, statistics and the betting odds," Daley said in a Sept. 28 *Times* column that his "hunch" was that the Giants would win the World Series.

Daley added that they were a "sound, solid ball club" with the ability to continually bounce back and win the "big game" they had to win. He also felt that Leo Durocher's "psychic" managerial powers at crucial moments would be a distinct advantage.

"Last but not least there is Willie the Wonder Mays," Daley also remarked. "He seems to symbolize the Giants."

Daley's hunch proved correct as The Giants swept the Indians in four games.

16. 1946 Red Sox

Members of Hall of Fame: 2.

The 1946 Red Sox were ranked fourth best among pennant winners that lost their World Series by one other study and 19th best overall by still another.

Ted Williams, the left fielder, batted .342, had 38 homers, and 123 RBI. Johnny Pesky at short batted

.335. Dom DiMaggio in center batted .316. First baseman Rudy York had 119 RBI. Second baseman Bobby Doerr had 116 RBI. Boo Ferriss was 25—6. Tex Hughson was 20—11.

John Drebinger previewed the World Series between these Red Sox and the St. Louis Cardinals on Oct. 5, 1946, in the *New York Times*:

"ST. LOUIS. OCT. 4. . . . Expert opinion leans almost unanimously toward the belief that the hard hitting and well-balanced American Leaguers will finish on top. Any difference of opinion focuses largely on whether it will go five, six or seven games. . . .

"When one examines comparative records, it becomes clear there is ample evidence to support this popular belief.

"The Red Sox swept through their American League campaign with a flourish, reminiscent of great Yankee teams of the past. . . .

"They started the season a vastly underrated club, but demonstrated in short order they meant to dominate the situation right through to the end, running away from the favored Yankees and a strong Tiger team.

"The Cardinals, on the other hand, went to the post in April with a club that, as subsequent events revealed, was considerably overrated. . . .

"On the attack, the glittering Bosox will enter the fray with a preponderance of strength on their side. They have the redoubtable Ted Williams spearheading a battle array that includes such exceptionally hard and consistent clouters as Rudy York, Dom DiMaggio, Bobby Doerr, Johnny Pesky, Wally Moses, Pinky Higgins and Hal Wagner. There is not much rest for any pitcher facing this lineup with nearly everyone in it clubbing in the vicinity of .300 or better. . . .

"In the American circuit, even top hurlers had to admit they never could find any real soft spots in the Red Sox battlefront. It was always a tough struggle from top to bottom, which is the way pitchers in that league used to feel about the Yankees a few years ago.

"On the defensive, the Red Sox also show an advantage, but not so pronounced. . . . The edge is there, if only because of superior pitching. . . .

"At several positions [the Sox] have some of the finest defensive players in the game. There are no flaws whatever on the inner line with York at first, Doerr at second, Pesky at short and the veteran Higgins at third.

"While the debatable Williams often leaves something to be desired as a fielder, his occasional lapses are more than offset by the brilliant Dom DiMaggio, one of the greatest defensive hawks of modern times, and either Moses or Tommy McBride. . . .

"Add to this the pitching, which many students value as high as 75 per cent of the game, and the Bosox do boast a heavy advantage. They have two top winning right handers in Dave Ferriss and Tex Hughson, an effective left hander in Mickey Harris and an additionally experienced right hander in Joe Dobson. . . .

"On the managerial side, the Sox again hold a slight edge. . . . Joe Cronin has been through the World Series mill before."

Drebinger concluded that the Sox should be able to win the series in five games.

Sports columnist Arthur Daley wrote about the surprising series that followed in the Oct. 15 *Times*:

"ST. LOUIS. OCT. 14. The Boston Red Sox have been the most prolonged favorites in World Series history. Ever since last May, when Joe Cronin's powerhouse was blasting the American League pennant race wide open, the fans have been feeling sorry for the National Leaguers who would have the misfortune to face the terrorizing Bosox contingent. . . .

"But here we are in the middle of October and, as Dizzy Dean might say, 'Them Bostons ain't kilt nobody dead yet.' In fact, they ain't even kilt them a little bit. When last observed, the St. Louis Cardinals were brimful of 'wim, wigor and witality.' They had battled the aloof and proud gentlemen from the Athens of America to a complete standstill.

"Unless the scoreboard lies shamefully, both teams now are tied in victories at three apiece. The seventh and deciding struggle is listed for tomorrow afternoon. . . .

"The Sox, as one wit remarked, were overbalanced. They had nothing but hitting and pitching. . . . But it didn't work out exactly that way at all. . . .

"Somehow or other, though, it seems inconceivable that there even should be a seventh and deciding game. . . .

On Oct. 16, the *Times'* John Drebinger reported the stunning final results:

"Bespectacled DiMaggio slapped a double off the right field wall, [Rip] Russell and [Catfish] Metkovich raced across the plate and the great conflict again was in a deadlock.

"This was to prove the highlight of the Bosox' bid to win a world title for Owner Tom Yawkey, who in 13 years had spent fabulous sums to produce a winner. DiMaggio, limping badly, left the field because of his pulled muscle and [Leon] Culberson ran for him. Leon did not have far to run. Williams, again utterly helpless before Cardinal pitching, fouled out to [Stan] Musial."

The Cardinals won the game 4-3, giving them a World Series few expected them to win, 4 games to 3.

17. 1976 Reds

Members of Hall of Fame: 2.

The 1976 Reds were ranked the third best team of all time by one study and in the Top 10 by another study.

The Reds had a record of 102-60 and finished 10 games ahead of the Dodgers in the National League West division race.

They placed high in four categories - tied for first in World Series Net, second in both Net Batting Average and Net Slugging Average and fourth in Net Runs.

Left fielder George Foster led the league in runs batted in with 121. He batted .306 and had 29 home runs. Joe Morgan, second base, batted .320, hit 27 homers and drove in 111 runs. Third baseman Pete Rose batted .323. Ken Griffey, the right fielder, batted .336. Cesar Geronimo, center field, batted .307.

Despite their great record, no Reds pitcher won more than 15 games. Gary Nolan was 15-9 with a 3.46 ERA. Pat Zachry was 14-7 with an ERA of 2.74. Don Gullett was 11-3 with an ERA of 3.00. Their best reliever was Rawly Eastwick, who had 26 saves and a record of 11-5 and an ERA of 2.08.

They swept the Yankees four games to none in the World Series.

They are almost the same team as the 1975 Reds, the 28th best team of all time, which were already profiled.

18. 1971 Orioles

Members of Hall of Fame: 3.

The Orioles' record was 101-57 and they captured the American League East division crown by 12 games.

Right fielder Merv Rettenmund led the team in batting with .318. Boog Powell, first base, had 22 home runs. Frank Robinson, who played the outfield, had 28 homers and 99 RBI. Third baseman Brooks Robinson had 20 home runs.

The Orioles had an amazing four 20-game winners! Dave McNally was 21-5 with an ERA of 2.89. Pat Dobson was 20-8 with an ERA of 2.90. Jim Palmer was 20-9 with an ERA of 2.68 and Mike Cuellar was also 20-9 with an ERA of 3.08. Eddie Watt had 11 saves with a 1.80 ERA.

The Orioles lost the World Series to the Pittsburgh Pirates four games to three. This was almost the same team as both the 1969 Orioles, the 12th best team of all time and best since World War II and as the 1970 Orioles, the seventh best since World War II. Both clubs were described previously.

19. 1947 Yankees

Members of Hall of Fame: 1.

The Yankees were 97-57 and finished 12 games ahead of the second-place Detroit Tigers.

Center fielder Joe DiMaggio led the team in hitting with a .315 batting average. He hit only 20 home runs but led the team. He had 97 RBI.

Tommy Henrich in right field led the team with 98 RBI. First baseman George McQuinn batted .304.

Spud Chandler led the league in ERA with 2.46. His record was 9-5. Allie Reynolds led the Yanks in wins. His record was 19-8 and his ERA was 3.20. Reliever Joe Page was 14-8 with 17 saves and a 2.48 ERA.

In the World Series, the Yanks beat the Brooklyn Dodgers four games to three.

20. 1950 Yankees

Members of Hall of Fame: 3.

The 1950 Yanks were ranked 23rd best of all time in one study.

The Yanks were 98-56 and finished three games ahead of second- place Detroit.

Shortstop Phil Rizzuto led the Yanks in batting with .324 and was named the A.L.'s MVP that season. Center fielder Joe DiMaggio led in homers with 32. He had 122 RBI and batted .301. Yogi Berra, the catcher, led in RBI with 124 while hitting 28 home runs and batted .322. Backup first baseman Johnny Mize got 25 homers in just 274 at bats.

Vic Raschi led the pitchers with a 21-8 record and a 4.00 ERA. Ed Lopat was 18-8 with an ERA of 3.47. Rookie Whitey Ford was 9-1 with an ERA of 2.81. Joe Page had 13 saves.

The Yankees swept the World Series with the Whiz Kid Phillies four games to none to finish tied for first in the World Series Net category.

This team had many of the same players as the 1953 Yankees, the 29th best team of all. That club is profiled earlier in this work.

Chapter 16
Where All 186 Pennant Winners Since 1901 Rank

We have employed our 11 criteria to determine where each of the 186 pennant winners from 1901 to date rank. The results appear in Table 17 below.

Table 17
How All 186 Pennant Winners Since 1901 Rank

1. 1927 New York Yankees 94.6
2. 1939 New York Yankees 90.7
3. 1929 Philadelphia Athletics 87.6
4. 1906 Chicago Cubs 86.2
5. 1902 Pittsburgh Pirates 86.0
6. 1936 New York Yankees 85.2
7. 1944 St. Louis Cardinals 84.1
8. 1931 Philadelphia Athletics 83.8
9. 1943 St. Louis Cardinals 81.8
10. 1932 New York Yankees 81.6
11. 1937 New York Yankees 80.6
12. 1969 Baltimore Orioles 79.8
13. 1910 Philadelphia Athletics 79.4
14. 1912 New York Giants 78.8
15. 1912 Boston Red Sox 78.7
16. 1954 Cleveland Indians 78.6
17. 1907 Chicago Cubs 78.5
18. 1905 New York Giants 78.4
19. 1942 St Louis Cardinals 76.7
20. 1904 New York Giants 76.3
21. 1953 Brooklyn Dodgers 76.0
22. 1909 Pittsburgh Pirates 75.3
23. 1911 Philadelphia Athletics 75.2
24. 1986 New York Mets 74.6

25.1942 New York Yankees 74.4
26.1941 New York Yankees 73.7
27.1938 New York Yankees 73.6
28.1975 Cincinnati Reds 73.3
29.1903 Boston Pilgrims (now Red Sox) 73.0
29.1953 New York Yankees 73.0
31.1948 Cleveland Indians 68.9
32.1970 Baltimore Orioles 68.6
331961 New York Yankees 68.1
34.1919 Cincinnati Reds 67.5
35.1910 Chicago Cubs 66.4
36.1928 New York Yankees 66.0
37.1913 New York Giants 65.5
37.1901 Pittsburgh Pirates 65.0
39.1923 New York Yankees 63.9
40.1984 Detroit Tigers 63.7
41.1931 St. Louis Cardinals 63.4
41.1955 Brooklyn Dodgers 63.4
41.1929 Chicago Cubs 63.4
44.1940 Cincinnati Reds 63.3
45.1930 Philadelphia Athletics 63.2
46.1935 Chicago Cubs 63.0
47.1911 New York Giants 62.1
48.1957 New York Yankees 61.6
48.1958 New York Yankees 61.6
50.1956 New York Yankees 61.4
51.1954 New York Giants 61.2
52.1946 Boston Red Sox 60.0
53.1934 Detroit Tigers 59.8
54.1976 Cincinnati Reds 59.7
55.1903 Pittsburgh Pirates 59.3
55.1918 Chicago Cubs 59.3
57.1971 Baltimore Orioles 59.2
58.1947 New York Yankees 59.0
59.1921 New York Yankees 58.8
60.1950 New York Yankees 58.6
60.1943 New York Yankees 58.6
62.1979 Baltimore Orioles 57.8
63.1951 New York Yankees 57.7
64.1925 Washington Nationals (later Senators) 57.6
65.1974 Los Angeles Dodgers 57.1
66.1922 New York Giants 57.0
67.1917 Chicago White Sox 56.6

68.1915 Boston Red Sox 56.3
69.1941 Brooklyn Dodgers 55.9
69.1935 Detroit Tigers 55.9
71.1920 Cleveland Indians 54.9
72.1925 Pittsburgh Pirates 54.6
72.1968 Detroit Tigers 54.6
74.1988 Oakland Athletics 54.0
75.1963 New York Yankees 53.9
76.1945 Chicago Cubs 52.9
77.1957 Milwaukee Braves 52.9
78.1955 New York Yankees 52.0
79.1933 Washington Nationals (later Senators) 51.6
80.1977 New York Yankees 51.4
81.1913 Philadelphia Athletics 51.3
82.1970 Cincinnati Reds 51.1
83.1917 New York Giants 50.6
84.1990 Oakland Athletics 50.2
85.1914 Philadelphia Athletics 50.1
85.1939 Cincinnati Reds 50.1
87.1989 Oakland Athletics 50.0
88.1952 New York Yankees 49.8
89.1949 New York Yankees 49.6
90.1977 Los Angeles Dodgers 49.2
91.1909 Detroit Tigers 48.3
92.1960 New York Yankees 48.2
93.1967 St. Louis Cardinals 48.1
94.1965 Minnesota Twins 47.7
94.1901 Chicago Stockings (now White Sox) 47.7
96.1966 Baltimore Orioles 46.5
97.1971 Pittsburgh Pirates 45.1
98.1946 St. Louis Cardinals 44.8
99.1934 St. Louis Cardinals 44.7
100.1928 St. Louis Cardinals 44.6
101.1969 New York Mets 44.5
102.1921 New York Giants 44.0
103.1958 Milwaukee Braves 43.6
103.1960 Pittsburgh Pirates 43.6
105.1933 New York Giants 43.3
105.1983 Baltimore Orioles 43.3
107.1985 St. Louis Cardinals 41.9
108.1924 Washington Nationals (later Senators) 41.8
109.1976 New York Yankees 41.6
110.1962 San Francisco Giants 41.4

111.1937 New York Giants 41.3
111.1924 New York Giants 41.3
111.1952 Brooklyn Dodgers 41.3
114.1919 Chicago White Sox 41.1
115.1908 Chicago Cubs 41.0
115.1978 New York Yankees 41.0
117.1930 St. Louis Cardinals 40.8
117.1949 Brooklyn Dodgers 40.8
119.1976 New York Yankees 40.5
119.1972 Cincinnati Reds 40.5
121.1948 Boston Braves 40.2
122.1991 Minnesota Twins 40.0
123.1951 New York Giants 39.4
124.1963 Los Angeles Dodgers 39.0
125.1962 New York Yankees 38.7
126.1920 Brooklyn Robins (later Dodgers) 38.6
127.1979 Pittsburgh Pirates 38.3
128.1936 New York Giants 37.7
129.1993 Philadelphia Phillies 37.7
130.1905 Philadelphia Athletics 37.6
131.1922 New York Yankees 37.5
131.1906 Chicago White Sox 37.5
133.1980 Kansas City Royals 37.4
133.1914 Boston Braves 37.4
135.1968 St. Louis Cardinals 37.2
136.1923 New York Giants 36.7
137.1904 Boston Pilgrims (now Red Sox) 36.2
138.1973 Oakland Athletics 35.9
139.1974 Oakland Athletics 35.8
140.1916 Brooklyn Robins (later Dodgers) 35.6
140.1926 New York Yankees 35.6
142.1915 Philadelphia Phillies 35.1
143.1940 Detroit Tigers 34.9
144.1992 Atlanta Braves 34.7
145.1978 Los Angeles Dodgers 34.3
146.1964 New York Yankees 33.2
147.1927 Pittsburgh Pirates 33.1
147.1965 Los Angeles Dodgers 33.1
149.1993 Toronto Blue Jays 32.9
150.1959 Chicago White Sox 32.7
151.1982 Milwaukee Brewers 32.4
151.1988 Los Angeles Dodgers 32.4
153.1947 Los Angeles Dodgers 31.7

153.1907 Detroit Tigers 31.7
153.1990 Cincinnati Reds 31.7
156.1926 St. Louis Cardinals 31.2
157.1975 Boston Red Sox 31.0
158.1918 Boston Red Sox 30.5
159.1972 Oakland Athletics 29.5
160.1992 Toronto Blue Jays 29.3
161.1981 Los Angeles Dodgers 28.9
162.1966 Los Angeles Dodgers 27.8
163.1950 Philadelphia Phillies 26.9
164.1986 Boston Red Sox 26.7
165.1981 New York Yankees 26.5
166.1961 Cincinnati Reds 26.1
167.1916 Boston Red Sox 25.3
168.1945 Detroit Tigers 24.6
169.1985 Kansas City Royals 24.5
170.1967 Boston Red Sox 24.4
171.1980 Philadelphia Phillies 24.0
172.1932 Chicago Cubs 23.4
173.1908 Detroit Tigers 23.0
174.1956 Brooklyn Dodgers 22.6
175.1938 Chicago Cubs 21.7
176.1964 St. Louis Cardinals 21.6
177.1991 Atlanta Braves 20.7
178.1984 San Diego Padres 20.0
178.1982 St. Louis Cardinals 20.0
180.1987 St. Louis Cardinals 19.3
181.1989 San Francisco Giants 18.0
182.1983 Philadelphia Phillies 17.3
183.1959 Los Angeles Dodgers 16.2
184.1944 St. Louis Browns 16.1
185.1987 Minnesota Twins 13.5
186.1973 New York Mets 13.2

Chapter 17
How Other Experts Voted

How does the evaluation of our computer compare with the ratings of the best teams of all time by other experts? We show this in Table 18 utilizing all the studies we have been able to find.

Table 18. The Top Baseball Teams of All Time According to Several Rankings

SPORTS

TEAM	HHHA	ASENG	HONIG	SINER	ILLUS	VASS
1927 Yankees	1	1	1	1	1	1
1939 Yankees	2	-	-	2	-	-
1929 Athletics	3	-	Top 10	4	7	-
1906 Cubs	4	2	Top 10	**	-	10
1902 Pirates	5	-	-	**	-	-
1936 Yankees	6	-	Top 10	10	4	11
1944 Cardinals	7	-	-	-	-	-
1931 Athletics	8	5	Top 10	2WSL*	-	2
1943 Cardinals	9	-	-	-	-	-
1932 Yankees	10	-	-	3	-	-
1937 Yankees	11	-	-	11	-	-
1969 Orioles	12	-	Top 10	5WSL	-	-
1910 Athletics	13	-	-	**	-	-
1912 Giants	14	-	-	**	-	-
1912 Red Sox	15	-	-	**	-	18
1954 Indians	16	-	-	1WSL	-	13
1907 Cubs	17	-	-	**	9	-
1905 Giants	18	-	-	**	3	-
1942 Cardinals	19	-	Top 10	5	17	6
1904 Giants	20	-	-	**	-	-

1953 Dodgers	21	-	Top 10	3WSL	-	-
1909 Pirates	22	-	-	**	-	9
1911 Athletics	23	-	Top 10	**	-	17
1986 Mets	24	**	**	7	-	**
1942 Yankees	25	-	-	-	-	-
1941 Yankees	26	-	-	13	-	-
1938 Yankees	27	-	-	18	-	-
1975 Reds	28	-	-	8	5	**
1903 Pilgrims	29	-	-	**	-	-
1953 Yankees	29	-	-	16	10	12
1885 White Stock's **		-	-	**	6	-
1914 Braves	-	-	-	**	20	-
1915 Red Sox	-	-	-	**	14	-
1919 White Sox	-	-	-	**	-	4
1920 Indians	-	-	-	24	-	-
1921 Giants	-	-	-	-	-	7
1923 Yankees	-	-	-	19	-	-
1924 Nationals	-	-	-	-	11	-
1928 Yankees	-	-	-	15	-	-
1929 Cubs	-	-	-	-	-	21
1930 Athletics	-	-	Top 10	12	-	-
1931 Cardinals	-	-	-	14	-	-
1934 Cardinals	-	-	-	-	13	20
1940 Reds	-	-	-	17	-	-
1946 Red Sox	16-WW***	-	-	4WSL	-	19
1947 Yankees	19-WW	-	-	-	-	-
1948 Indians	7-WW	-	-	-	-	-
1950 Yankees	20-WW	-	-	23	-	-
1951 Yankees	-	-	-	22	-	-
1954 Giants	15-WW	-	-	-	15	-
1955 Dodgers	11-WW	8	-	21	18	8
1956 Yankees	14-WW	-	-	-	-	-
1957 Yankees	12-WW	-	-	-	-	-
1957 Braves	-	-	-	-	-	14
1958 Yankees	12-WW	-	-	-	-	-
1961 Yankees	9-WW	6	Top 10	6	2	5
1967 Cardinals	-	-	-	-	-	15
1968 Tigers	-	-	-	25	-	-
1969 Mets	-	-	-	-	19	-
1970 Orioles	8-WW	4	-	9	16	3
1971 Orioles	18-WW	-	-	-	-	-
1973 Athletics	-	7	-	-	-	16
1974 Athletics	-	-	-	-	8	**

1976 Reds	17-WW	3	Top 10	-	-	**
1984 Tigers	10-WW	-	**	20	-	**
1989 Athletics	-	**	**	**	12	**

* - WSL - World Series Loser. Siner lists these five teams separately from teams that won the World Series.

** - Teams not rated for this year either because study was done subsequently or author arbitrarily omitted this year.

*** - WW indicates that this team was not among the Top 30 but held the indicated rank among post-World War II teams.

SOURCES:

HHH - This study's Top 30.

AASENG - Aaseng, Nathan. *Baseball's Greatest Teams.* Mankato, Minn.: Lerner Publications, 1984.

HONIG - Honig, Donald. *Baseball's Ten Greatest Teams.* New York: Macmillan, 1982.

SINER - Siner, Howard. *Sweet Seasons: Baseball's Greatest Teams Since 1920.* New York: Pharos Books, 1988.

SPORTS ILLUS - Bauer, David, ed. *Sports Illustrated Presents Baseball's 20 Greatest Teams of All Time.* New York: Time Inc. Magazine Company, 1991.

VASS - Vass, George. "Baseball's All-time Ten Best Teams." *Baseball Digest*, September, 1974, pp. 28-37.

The only thing on which we all agree is that the 1927 New York Yankees were the greatest team of all time.

Most of the other experts agree with our contention that the 1929 Athletics, 1906 Cubs, 1936 Yankees, 1931 Athletics, 1942 Cardinals and 1953 Yankees are among the all-time best. But of our Top 10, no one else even listed the 1902 Pirates and the 1943 and 1944 Cardinals. In our second ten, no one else listed the 1910

Athletics and the 1904 and 1912 Giants. In our third ten, no one else ranked the 1942 Yankees and 1903 Pilgrims (now Red Sox).

Three teams which did not make our Top 30 were ranked highly by four of the other experts. They were the 1970 Orioles, which we ranked 32nd; the 1961 Yankees, which we ranked 33rd; and the 1955 Dodgers, which we ranked 41st.

Five other teams not included in our Top 30 were ranked by two of the other experts. They were (with our ranking in parentheses): 1930 Athletics (45), 1946 Red Sox (52), 1976 Reds (54), 1934 Cardinals (99) and 1973 Athletics (137).

In addition, 22 other teams that were not in our Top 30 were named by one - but no other - expert as one of the best of all time.

This shows pretty clearly how much difference there is between subjective selections and the mathematical ones we made.

At the same time, it must be conceded that others may weight the criteria we used differently. Several felt that a team's World Series performance must be given considerable weight. We gave it only 5%.

Others argued, like Connie Mack once did, that a team must be considered over time - not just in one season. Our rankings, of course, were strictly based upon the performance during a single season.

It also appears that the others pretty much ruled out some of the very early teams (one ruled out teams that played before 1920) and the World War II teams, neither of which we did.

PART II
THE 30 WORST TEAMS
OF ALL TIME

Chapter 18
The Criteria for Selecting the Worst Teams

Again, we considered only teams that had played since 1901 and only teams that had finished last in their league or in their division since division play started in 1969. This means we looked at a total of 243 teams (including ties).

We used a technique similar to the one we used to select the best teams, but in this case we used only four criteria.

Two of these were Net Batting Average and Net Earned Run Average. The weights for these two criteria were developed by running a multiple regression with Percentage of Games Won as the dependent variable. As can be seen by the weights, pitching is much more important than batting.

The other two criteria used were Percentage of Games Won and Games Behind Second to Last Place Team.

In Tables 16 through 19, we show the 10 worst teams in each of four characteristics.

Percentage of Games Won

Table 19
Percentage of Games Won (40%)

1. 1916 Philadelphia Athletics .235
2. 1935 Boston Braves .248
3. 1962 New York Mets .250

4. 1904 Washington Nationals (later Senators) .252
5. 1919 Philadelphia Athletics .257
6. 1952 Pittsburgh Pirates .273
7. 1909 Washington Nationals (later Senators) .276
8. 1942 Philadelphia Phillies .278
9. 1932 Boston Red Sox .279
9. 1939 St. Louis Browns .279
9. 1941 Philadelphia Phillies .279

No team ever won a lower percentage of its games than the 1916 Philadelphia Athletics who won only .235 of their games. Next worse were the 1935 Pittsburgh Pirates, followed by the expansion 1962 New York Mets, the 1904 Washington Nationals and, fifth worst, the 1919 Athletics.

Games Behind Second To Last Place Team

Table 20
Games Behind Second to Last Place Team (25%)

1. 1916 Philadelphia Athletics 40
2. 1969 San Diego Padres 29
3. 1979 Toronto Blue Jays 28.5
4. 1988 Atlanta Braves 27
5. 1935 Boston Braves 26
6. 1938 Philadelphia Phillies 24.5
7. 1988 Baltimore Orioles 23.5
7. 1904 Washington Nationals (later Senators) 23.5
9. 1952 Pittsburgh Pirates 22.5
10. 1925 Boston Red Sox 21

The 1916 Athletics were bad. Really bad. Not only did they have the lowest percentage ever of games won, but they also finished further behind the next to last team than any other club; an unbelievable 40 games behind the seventh place team in 1916.

The 1969 expansion San Diego Padres were second worst; the 1979 expansion Toronto Blue Jays, third worst; the 1988 Atlanta Braves, fourth worst; and the 1935 Boston Braves, fifth worst.

Batting

Table 21
Net Batting Average (x1,000) (10%)

1. 1911 St. Louis Browns -34
2. 1920 Philadelphia Athletics -31
2. 1979 Oakland Athletics -31
4. 1981 Toronto Blue Jays -30
5. 1922 Boston Braves -29
6. 1965 New York Mets -28
7. 1924 Boston Braves -27
8. 1925 Boston Red Sox -26
8. 1927 Boston Red Sox -26
8. 1932 Boston Red Sox -26
8. 1940 Philadelphia Phillies -26
8. 1963 New York Mets -26
8. 1974 San Diego Padres -26
8. 1977 Oakland Athletics -26
8. 1983 Seattle Mariners -26

The 1911 St. Louis Browns were the poorest hitting last place team in history, batting 34 points lower than the American League average in 1911. The 1920 Philadelphia Athletics and the 1979 Oakland Athletics were next worst, followed by the expansion 1981 Toronto Blue Jays. The 1922 Boston Braves were fifth worst.

Net Earned Run Average

Table 22
Net Earned Run Average (25%)

1. 1930 Philadelphia Phillies +1.74
2. 1911 Boston Rustlers (later Braves) +1.69

3. 1928 Philadelphia Phillies +1.54
4. 1954 Philadelphia Athletics +1.46
5. 1927 Philadelphia Phillies +1.44
6. 1939 St. Louis Browns +1.39
6. 1915 Philadelphia Athletics +1.39
8. 1937 St. Louis Browns +1.38
9. 1926 Philadelphia Phillies +1.35
10. 1923 Philadelphia Phillies +1.31

The last place team with the worst pitching in history was the 1930 Philadelphia Phillies whose ERA was 1.74 points higher than the average for the NL that year. Next worst were the 1911 Boston Rustlers. Then came the 1928 Phillies, the 1954 Philadelphia Athletics, and the 1927 Phillies.

Chapter 19
The 30 Worst Teams of All Time

In Table 23 are listed the 30 worst baseball teams of all time.

Table 23
The 30 Worst Baseball Teams of All Time

1. 1916 Philadelphia Athletics 8.8
2. 1919 Philadelphia Athletics 10.0
3. 1904 Washington Nationals (later Senators) 10.1
4. 1935 Boston Braves 10.5
5. 1962 New York Mets 10.7
6. 1952 Pittsburgh Pirates 11.0
7. 1911 Boston Rustlers (later Braves) 13.8
8. 1938 Philadelphia Phillies 15.8
9. 1941 Philadelphia Phillies 17.0
10. 1939 St. Louis Browns 17.4
11. 1909 Washington Nationals (later Senators) 17.6
12. 1942 Philadelphia Phillies 17.7
13. 1939 Philadelphia Phillies 17.9
14. 1915 Philadelphia Athletics 18.4
15. 1928 Philadelphia Phillies 20.8
16. 1925 Boston Red Sox 21.8
17. 1911 St. Louis Browns 22.8
18. 1945 Philadelphia Blue Jays (now Phillies) 23.0
19. 1969 San Diego Padres 23.1
19. 1910 St. Louis Browns 23.1
21. 1903 Washington Nationals (later Senators) 23.2
22. 1937 St. Louis Browns 24.2
23. 1926 Boston Red Sox 24.3
24. 1943 Philadelphia Athletics 25.7
25. 1961 Philadelphia Phillies 25.9
26. 1932 Boston Red Sox 26.0
26. 1963 New York Mets 26.0

28.1979 Toronto Blue Jays 26.2
29.1909 Boston Doves (later Braves) 26.5
30.1953 Pittsburgh Pirates 28.0

A Word About the Cleveland Spiders

Actually, if we had not decided that only statistical records starting in 1901 should be used, the worst team of all time would almost certainly have been one that does not show up in this table. That team was the 1899 Cleveland Spiders, also known as the Exiles, because they had to play most of their games on the road when Cleveland fans stopped attending their games.

The inept Spiders set almost every conceivable record for futility. During 1899, they won only 20 games and lost 134. They finished an unbelievable 84 games behind first-place Brooklyn. In September, they won only one game and lost 27, the worst record for one month in baseball history and they had losing streaks of 24 (still the record), 16 and 14 games.

The Cleveland team had actually won more games than it lost the previous year, but was in the unfortunate situation of being owned by the same man as owned the St. Louis Cardinals. The owner stripped the Spiders of all its talent in favor of the Cards.

About the 30 Worst Since 1901

The city of Philadelphia dominates the Worst 30 list with 11 teams, seven Phillie clubs and four Athletic squads. The St. Louis Browns also appear on the list four times, even though they changed their name and moved to Baltimore in 1953.

The Boston Braves, Boston Red Sox, New York Mets and Washington Nationals (later Senators) franchises each appear on the list three times.

Except for expansion teams, only three post-World War II teams are on the list: the 1952 and 1953 Pitts-

burgh Pirates and the 1961 Philadelphia Phillies, all
National League teams.

Chapter 20
The Two Worst Teams of All:
the 1916 and 1919 Athletics

The Worst Team of All: the 1916 Athletics

In our research, we found two books (*On a Clear Day They Could See Seventh Place* by George Robinson and Charles Salzberg, 1991; and *Baseball's Worst Teams* by Nathan Aaseng, 1984) and three articles naming the worst teams of all time. All five included the 1916 A's on their lists. (See Table 25.)

Connie Mack owned and managed the Philadelphia Athletics for 50 seasons, from 1901, when the American League started, through 1950. During those 50 years, he led the team to seven pennants and five world championships. His 1929 A's were the third best team of all time. His 1931 A's were the eighth best; his 1910 A's, 13th best and his 1911 A's, 23rd best.

Yet, his 1916 A's were the worst team of all time. His 1919 team was the second worst; his 1915 team, 14th worst and his 1943 team, 24th worst.

In 1914, the A's won the AL pennant for the fourth time in five years but when the team failed to win the World Series for a second consecutive year, Mack dismantled his club. Halfway through the 1915 season, only four regulars remained from the 1914 team and before the 1916 season, Mack got rid of three of them.

In 1916, six AL teams finished with records of .500 or better and the seventh-place team won .494 of its games. The A's won only 36 and lost 117, a .235 winning percentage.

Despite their awful record, the A's had one good pitcher, Bullet Joe Bush, who won 15 of the 36 games won by the A's, eight by shutouts. Jack Nabors lost a record 19 games in a row. Tom Sheehan was 1 and 16.

The "$10 Infield" was "led" by shortstop Whitey Witt, who committed 78 errors. Third baseman Charlie Pick made 42 errors, tops for third baseman in the league. Nap Lajoie, already 41 years old, played second.

It was Connie Mack's second of seven consecutive basement finishes. Mack would set a record with 17 last place teams.

Second Worst: 1919 Athletics

This is another in the string of seven straight last place teams for Connie Mack and some of the players who had been on the worst team of all, the 1916 A's, were still around.

Probably because they thought they had already given the 1916- 1919 Athletics all the "credit" they deserved, only one of the five other experts listed the 1919 A's among the worst of all time.

This team's record was 36 and 104. They finished 52 games out of first and 20 out of seventh. The team's ERA was 4.26, nearly a full run higher than the second worst staff in the league that year. The team batting average, .244, was the lowest in both leagues.

The pitching staff had only one shutout all year, by Tom "Shotgun" Rogers who won only four games during the season.

Chapter 21
The Rest of the Worst

Third Worst Team: 1904 Nationals
(later Senators)

Three of the five studies of the worst teams included the 1904 Washington Nationals on their lists.

This was one of four new teams created when the American League came into being in 1901. Their owners were not very successful in signing established players for the team.

The one National League star the Nationals had signed, "Big Ed" Delahanty, died in an accident halfway through the 1903 season. He was later voted into the Hall of Fame.

The Nationals' top batter was first baseman Jake Stahl who hit .262 and led the team in runs batted in with 50. Rookie Joe Cassidy was the only other infielder to hit above .218.

Three pitchers had more than 20 losses. Case Patten was 14—23. (The Nationals were shut out in nine of the games Patten started.) John "Happy" Townsend led the league with 26 losses against 5 wins and Albert "Beany" Jacobson was 6-23.

The team lost its first 13 games and ended up winning only 38 and losing 113. They had the lowest fielding and batting averages and the highest ERA in the league.

While the team won 38 games, Jack Chesbro of the

New York Giants won 41 games all by himself!

The Nationals ended up 55 1/2 games out of first and 24 out of seventh.

Manager Malachi Kittredge was fired as a result of the team's poor start. Thus, his managing career started and ended with the Nationals that year; his record: one win, 16 losses and a tie.

He was replaced with a playing manager, Patsy Donovan, who already had experience, managing the St. Louis Cardinals to a last place National League finish in 1903.

Fourth Worst Team: 1935 Boston Braves

Outfielder Wally Berger made it difficult for this team to lose by leading the National League with 34 homers and 130 runs batted in, but they still found a way.

If Berger were not enough of a problem for a losing team, it also had on its roster two future Hall of Famers, Babe Ruth and Rabbit Maranville. Ruth, one of the greatest sluggers of all time, was over the hill at 40 years of age and hit only six home runs for the Braves before hanging up his spikes in midseason.

The Braves won 38 and lost 115. They won only 13 games on the road. They lost 15 straight in the middle of the season. Ben Cantwell won 4 and lost 25. He was the majors' last 25-game loser. Ed Brandt lost 19. Bob Smith lost 18.

Fifth Worst: 1962 Mets

This is another favorite "worst team." All four of the experts who did their studies after 1982 named the '62 New York Mets to their lists.

This was the expansion Mets' first year. They opened with nine losses and ended up winning 40 games and losing 120. The 120 is still a modern major league record for losses in a season. They had losing strings of 17, 13 and 11 games under 71-year-old Manager Casey Stengel.

Pitcher Craig Anderson lost 16 games in a row and ended up 3 and 17. Roger Craig was 10 and 24. He lost 18 in a row. Bob Miller lost his first 12. Al Jackson was 8 and 20. Jay Hook was 8 and 19.

"Marvelous Marv" Throneberry played first and "Choo Choo" Coleman was the catcher, but the Mets did have some quality players, including Richie Ashburn, Gil Hodges, and Frank Thomas, who hit 34 homers. Unfortunately, Ashburn had already played in 15 campaigns and Hodges was 38 years old and neither was the player he once was.

The 1962 Mets were last in the National League in batting, fielding and pitching (ERA).

They, however, did attract almost one million fans, more than any other last-place team in baseball history.

The Mets held onto last place for three more years. During their first four seasons, the Mets lost 452 games, an average of 113 per season.

Sixth Worst: 1952 Pirates

Two of the other five experts included the 1952 Pittsburgh Pirates on their worst lists.

The Pirates' record was 42 and 112, 54 1/2 games out of first and 22 1/2 out of seventh. The Pirate pitchers walked 615 men while striking out just 564. Sixteen different men started for the Pirates during the season.

Ralph Kiner made it hard for this team to lose by hitting 37 home runs. Gus Bell hit 16. But pitchers Murry Dickson, Howie Pollet and Bob Friend won only a combined total of 28 games among them.

Catcher Joe Garagiola described the team as "in the ninth year of General Manager Branch Rickey's latest five-year plan."

Seventh Worst: 1911 Rustlers (later the Braves)

This Braves team (known as the Rustlers for the 1911 season) also made losing look easy, even though they had four regulars who batted over .300, including right fielder Doc Miller, at .333. But pitching saved the day with Buster Brown pacing the staff with an 8—18 record, and Al Mattern was not far behind with a mark of 4 up and 15 down.

Eighth Worst: 1938 Phillies

First baseman Phil Weintraub batted .311, but it did not help much. Hugh Mulcahy led the league in losses with 20 against only 10 wins and Claude Passeau was close at 11—18. Al Hollingsworth (no relation to the author) was 7 and 18.

Ninth Worst: 1941 Phillies

The team was led by first baseman Nick Etten who batted .311, with 79 runs batted in. Left fielder Danny Litwhiler batted .305 and led the team with 18 homers. The best pitchers each had nine wins. They were Johnny Podgajny at 9 and 12 and Tommy Hughes at 9 and 14. In the 27 seasons from 1919 through 1945, the Phillies finished either last or seventh 23 times. From 1919 to 1955, when the Athletics left Philadelphia, the two teams shared the cellars in the two leagues nine times.

10th Worst: 1939 Browns

Two of the other five studies of the worst teams had the 1939 St. Louis Browns on their lists, and with good reason.

These Browns finished 64 1/2 games out of first, an American League record. They won 43 and lost 111.

Like some other bad teams, they had some excellent players, including first baseman George McQuinn and third baseman Harlond Clift. The two hit 35 home runs together and 178 RBI. McQuinn batted .316.

Howver, no pitcher won more than nine games, a number shared by each of their two stars, Jack Kramer and Vern Kennedy.

The St. Louis Browns went 42 years without a pennant and were league champions only once in their 51-year history.

11th Worst: 1909 Nationals (later Senators)

This team hit a total of nine home runs all season. And like the two previous teams in this list, it had to overcome a sizeable "handicap" to be one of the worst teams - on its roster was the immortal Walter "Big Train" Johnson, still in his prime. He had 13 wins and 25 losses, but a 2.21 ERA, giving some indication of the sort of batting support he must have received. Bob Groom went 7—26 to lead the American League in losses and Dolly Gray was 5-19.

And whatever happened to Walter Johnson? He won more than 20 games for the Nationals each year for the next 10 years. He won 36 in 1913. Again in 1924 and 1925, he won more than 20, making a total of 12 years with 20 or more wins.

12th Worst: 1942 Phillies

This team was included on the worst lists of two of the other experts. It was composed of the same people by and large who made up the ninth worst team.

The team won 42 and lost 109, finishing 62 1/2 games out of first making the assesment a simple one.

Left fielder Danny Litwhiler led the Phillies with

nine homers, 56 RBI and batted .271. In the middle of the infield were future Big League managers Bobby Bragan and Danny Murtaugh. A part-timer in the outfield was Lloyd "Big Poison" Waner. Ruby Melton lost 20.

13th Worst: 1939 Phillies

These Phillies won 45 and lost 106 and finished 18 games behind the seventh-place Bees (as the Braves were then known).

The most home runs any Phillies batsman was 9. They did however, have three .300 hitters: left fielder Morrie Arnovich with .324, first baseman Gus Suhr with .318, and catcher Spud Davis with .307. Arnovich also led the team in RBI with 67.

Kirby Higbe was their leading pitcher with a record of 10-14 and an ERA of 4.85. Hugh Mulcahy had the most losses. His record was 9-16 with a 4.99 ERA.

14th Worst: 1915 Athletics

The Athletics' record was 43 and 109 and they finished 14 games behind the seventh-place Indians.

Their batting leader was first baseman Stuffy McInnis with .314. Left fielder Rube Oldring led in homers with 6. Nap Lajoie, second base, led in RBI with 61.

Weldon Wyckoff led the league in losses. His record was 10-22 with an ERA of 3.52. He was also the Athletics' biggest winner. Rube Bressler was 4-17 with a 5.20 ERA. Bullet Joe Bush was 5-15 with a 4.14 ERA.

15th Worst: 1928 Phillies

This team was 43-109 finishing 6 1/2 games behind the seventh- place Braves.

Left fielder Freddy Leach led the team in hitting with .304. First baseman Don Hurst was the home run leader with 19. Pinky Whitney, third base, batted .301 and led the team in RBI with 103. It was Chuck Klein's first year. He played right field and batted .360 but had only 253 at bats.

Ray Benge led the pitchers with a record of 8-18 and a 4.55 ERA. He also had the most losses. Jimmy Ring was 4-17 and posted a 6.40 ERA. Les Sweetland was 3-15 with a 6.58 ERA. Russ Miller was 0-12 with a 5.42 ERA.

The team ERA was a generous 5.52.

16th Worst: 1925 Red Sox

These Red Sox were 47-105 and finished 21 games behind the seventh-place Yankees. (These are the same Yankees who two years later became the greatest baseball team of all time!)

The leading batter was right fielder Ike Boone with .330. He also led in RBI with 68. The home run leader with 11 was Phil Todt, the first baseman. Left fielder Roy Carlyle batted .326.

The leading Red Sox pitcher was Ted Wingfield with 12 wins and 19 losses with a 3.96 ERA. Howard Ehmke, who later pitched for the 1929 Athletics (third best team of all time), was 9-20 with a 3.73 ERA. Rookie Red Ruffing - who like many other BoSox, would later have a very long, distinguished career with the Yankees - posted a 9-18 record with a 5.02 ERA.

17th Worst: 1911 Browns

The Browns were 45-107 and finished 18 games behind the seventh-place Washington Nationals (they became the Senators later).

Their leading batter was second baseman Frank LaPorte with .314. He also led the team in RBI with 82. Paul Meloan, an outfielder, led the team in homers with 3.

Jack Powell led the league in losses with 19. He won eight and recorded an ERA of 3.29. Joe Lake had the most wins for the team. His record was 10-15 with an ERA of 4.30. Barney Pelty was 7-15 with an ERA of 2.83.

The team ERA was 3.83 while the American League's was 3.34.

18th Worst: 1945 Blue Jays (now Phillies)

The Blue Jays, as the Phillies were nicknamed in 1945 and 1946, were truly for the birds finishing 46-108, 15 games behind the seventh-place Cincinnati Reds.

The top batter was Jimmy Wasdell, the first baseman, with .300. Vince DiMaggio, center field, led in home runs with 19 and in RBI with 84.

Dick Barrett led the league in losses. His record was 7-20 with a 5.43 ERA. Andy Karl led the team in wins with a record of 9-8 and an ERA of 2.99. He also had 15 saves. Charley Schanz was 4-15 with a 4.35 ERA.

19th Worst: 1969 Padres

This was the expansion Padres' first year. They were 52-110, finishing 29 games behind the fifth-place Houston Astros in the six-team National League West division. In fact, their record was so bad that they permitted every other team in their division to finish .500 or better.

Their top batter, left fielder Al Ferrara, hit only .260. The top home run and RBI man was first baseman Nate Colbert with 24 and 66 respectively. Right Fielder Ollie Brown had 20 homers.

Clay Kirby led the league in losses. His record was 7-20 and his ERA was 3.79. Two pitchers tied for most wins with eight: Joe Niekro, 8-17 with a 3.70 ERA and Al Santorini, 8-14 with an ERA of 3.94. Tommy Sisk was 2-13 with a 4.78 ERA.

20th Worst: 1911 Browns

The Browns were 47-107 and 20 1/2 games behind the seventh-place Washington Nationals. (see 17th worst team)

Shortstop Bobby Wallace led in batting with .258. No one hit more than two home runs. Their leading RBI man was left fielder George Stone with 40.

Joe Lake led the team in wins with 11. He lost 17 and had a respectable ERA of 2.20. Bill Bailey had most losses with a 3-18 record and an ERA of 3.32.

The team ERA was 3.09 while the American League ERA was 2.53.

21st Worst: 1903 Nationals (later Senators)

The Nationals were 43-94 and 17 games behind the seventh-place Chicago White Stockings (now the White Sox).

Their leading hitter was their third baseman, Bill Coughlin who hit .251. Jimmy Ryan, center field, led them in homers with 7. Kip Selbach, left field, led them in RBI with 49.

Two pitchers tied for most losses for the team with 22 each. Casey Patten was 11-22 with an ERA of 3.60. Al Orth was 10-22 with a 4.34 ERA. Patten had the most wins. Jack Townsend was 2-11 with an ERA of 4.76. Highball Wilson was 7-18 with a 3.31 ERA.

The team batting average was .231; the American League's, .256. The team's ERA was 3.82; the league's, 2.95.

22nd Worst: 1937 Browns

The Browns were 46-108 and 9 1/2 games behind the Athletics.

Their leading hitter was right fielder Beau Bell with a .340 average. The top home run man was third baseman Harlond Clift with 29. He also led the team in RBI with 118 and batted .306. Also batting .300 or better were center fielder Sammy West at .328 and left fielder Joe Vosmik with a .325 average.

In addition, the Browns also had a reserve, Ethan Allen, who hit .316 in 320 at bats. The team batted .285, higher than the American League's .281 — a rare feat for a last place team. They also led the league in doubles.

But pitching was the Browns undoing. Their team ERA was a staggering 6.00 compared with the league's 4.62. Jim Walkup won the most games. His record was 9-12 with a 7.36 ERA.

Jack Hogsett had the most losses. He was 6-19 with an ERA of 6.29. Jack Knott had a record of 8-18 with an ERA of 4.89 - outstanding for this team. Oral Hildebrand was 8-17 with a 5.14 ERA.

23rd Worst: 1926 Red Sox

The Red Sox were 46-107, 15 1/2 games behind the seventh-place Browns.

Their leading hitter was right fielder Baby Doll Jacobson with .305. Phil Todt, first base, led in homers with 7. Jacobson and Todt tied for most RBI with 69.

Paul Zahniser led the league in losses. His record was 6-18 with a 4.97 ERA. Ted Wingfield won the most games for the Sox. His record was 11-16 with an ERA of 4.44. Future Hall of Famer Red Ruffing was 6-15 with a 4.39 ERA. Hal Wiltse was 8-15 with a 4.22 ERA. Howard Ehmke was 3-10 with an ERA of 5.46.

24th Worst: 1943 Athletics

The A's were 49-105 and 20 games behind the seventh-place Boston Red Sox.

Their leading batter was left fielder Bobby Estalella with .259. He also led the team in homers with 11. First baseman Dick Siebert led the team in RBI with 72.

Lum Harris led the American League in losses. His record was 7-21. His ERA was 4.20. Jesse Flores led the team in wins with 12. He had 14 losses with an ERA of 3.11. Roger Wolff was 10-15 with an ERA of 3.54. Don Black was 6-16 with a 4.20 ERA.

25th Worst: 1961 Phillies

The Phillies were 47-107. They finished 17 behind the Cubs, who were seventh.

The Phillies' leading batter was left fielder Johnny Callison with .266. Don Demeter, the right fielder, led in homers with 20. He also led in RBI with 68.

Art Mahaffey led the National League in losses. His record was 11-19. His 11 wins led the team. His ERA was 4.10. John Buzhardt was 6-18 with a 4.49 ERA. Frank Sullivan was 3-16 with an ERA of 4.29. Robin Roberts - who in 1952 went 28—23 in each of 1953, 1954 and 1955 - was 1-10 with an ERA of 5.85.

26th Worst: 1932 Red Sox

The Red Sox were 43-111 and 7 1/2 games behind the seventh-place White Sox.

Surprisingly, their first baseman, Dale Alexander, led the league in batting at .367. He had arrived in a trade with Detroit early in the season. Smead Jolley, the left fielder, led the team in both home runs and RBI with 18 and 99 respectively. He batted .309.

Bob Kline led the pitchers with a record of 11-13 and an ERA of 5.28. Bob Weiland had the most losses going 6-16 with a 4.51 ERA. Ed Durham was 6-13 with a 3.80 ERA. Danny MacFayden was 1-10 with a 5.10 ERA.

26th Worst: 1963 Mets

This was the expansion Mets' second year. In their first year, 1962, they were the fifth worst team of all time. In 1963, they were 51-111, 15 games behind Houston.

Their leading hitter was second baseman Ron Hunt with a .272 batting average. Center fielder Jim Hickman was their home run leader with 17. Frank Thomas, in left, led in RBI with 60. The once great Duke Snider was on the team. He batted .243 with 14 homers and 45 RBI playing right field for the hapless "Let's Go's."

Roger Craig who led the National League in losses was 5-22 with an ERA of 3.78. Al Jackson had the team's most wins posting a 13-17 record with a 3.96 ERA. Tracy Stallard was 6-17 with a 4.71 ERA. Jay Hook was 4-14 with a 5.48 ERA. Galen Cisco was 7-15 with a 4.34 ERA.

28th Worst: 1979 Blue Jays

This was the third year for the expansion Toronto Blue Jays, who fell to new depths. They were 53-109, 28 1/2 games behind the Indians, who finished sixth in the American League East division.

Their leading hitter was shortstop Alfredo Griffin with .287. First baseman John Mayberry led them in homers with 21 and in RBI with 74.

Phil Huffman had the most losses in the league. He was 6-18 with an ERA of 5.77. Tom Underwood led the Jays in wins. He was 9-16 with a 3.69 ERA.

29th Worst: 1909 Doves (later Braves)

The Doves had a record of 45-108 and finished 9 1/2 games behind the seventh-place Cardinals.

Their leading batters were Ginger Beaumont, the center fielder, and Roy Thomas, the left fielder, both with .263. Right fielder Beals Becker led in homers with 6. Beaumont also led in RBI with 60.

Cecil Ferguson led the National League in losses. His record was 5-23 with an ERA of 3.73. Al Mattern led the team in wins. His record was 16-20 with an ERA of 2.85. Kirby White was 6-13 with a 3.22 ERA. The team ERA was 3.20, but the league's was 2.59.

30th Worst: 1953 Pirates

The Pirates record was 50-104. They finished 15 games behind the Chicago Cubs, who were seventh.

Third Baseman Danny O'Connell led the team in batting with .294. Left fielder Frank Thomas led the team in home runs with 30. He also led in RBI with 102. Hal Rice, a reserve outfielder, batted .310 but batted only 294 times.

Murry Dickson had the most losses in the National League with 19. He won 10 and posted a 4.53 ERA. He also had the team's most wins. Johnny Lindell was 5-16 with an ERA of 4.71 before being traded to the Phillies.

Paul LaPalme was 8-16 with an ERA of 4.59. Bob Hall was 3-12 with an ERA of 5.39. Rookie Roy Face posted a record of 6-8 and an ERA of 6.58. Later, he would lead the league in saves in 1958, 1960 and 1961.

The team ERA was 5.22; the league's, 4.29.

Teams Missing From Worst List

The most notable omission from the list of the 30 worst teams of all time is the New York Yankees, the team which dominated the Top 30 list with nine different clubs.

Also missing were the Giants, whether from New York

or San Francisco, who appeared three times on the best list, and the St. Louis Cardinals, who were also on the best list three times.

Other teams missing on the 30 worst list were the Baltimore Orioles (twice on the best list), the Chicago Cubs (twice on the best list), the Cleveland Indians (once on the best list) and the Brooklyn (now Los Angeles) Dodgers (once on the best list).

The only two original franchises that appear on neither the best nor worst lists are the Detroit Tigers and Chicago White Sox.

Chapter 22
The Worst Teams According to Other Experts

We were able to find five other books and articles listing the worst baseball teams of all time. All, unlike our mathematical study, were based upon the author's judgement.

How these five ranked the worst teams of all time compared with how our computer did is shown in Table 25.

Table 25
How Our Ratings of Worst Teams Compare with
Those of Other Experts

TEAM	HHH	SALZ.	AASENG	MUEL.	ALLEN	OLBER.
1916 Athletics	1	Worst 1911-20	3	Worst 4	2	1
1919 Athletics	2	-	-	-	-	7
1904 Nationals	3	Worst 1901-10	5	-	-	-
1935 Braves	4	Worst 1931-40	-	Worst 4	2	3
1962 Mets	5	Worst 1961-70	2	Worst 4	*	4
1952 Pirates	6	Worst 1951-60	-	-	*	5
1911 Rustlers	7	-	-	-	-	-
1938 Phillies	8	-	-	-	-	-
1941 Phillies	9	-	-	-	-	-
1939 Browns	10	-	4	-	-	6
1909 Nationals	11	-	-	-	-	-
1942 Phillies	12	Worst 1941-50	-	-	-	8
1939 Phillies	13	-	-	-	-	-
1915 Athletics	14	-	-	-	-	-
1928 Phillies	15	Worst 1921-30	-	-	-	-
1925 Red Sox	16	-	-	-	-	-
1911 Browns	17	-	-	-	-	-

Team	HHH	SALZ	AASENG	MUEL	ALLEN	OLBER
1945 Blue Jays	18	-	-	-	-	-
1969 Padres	19	-	-	-	*	-
1910 Browns	19	-	-	-	-	-
1903 Nationals	21	-	-	-	-	-
1937 Browns	22	-	-	-	-	-
1926 Red Sox	23	-	-	-	-	-
1943 Athletics	24	-	-	-	-	-
1961 Phillies	25	-	6	-	*	9
1932 Red Sox	26	-	7	-	-	-
1963 Mets	26	-	-	-	*	-
1979 Blue Jays	28	Worst 1971-80	-	-	*	-
1909 Doves	29	-	-	-	-	-
1953 Pirates	30	-	-	-	*	-
1899 Spiders	*	Worst 1891-00	1	Worst 4	1	-
1906 Beaneaters	-	-	-	-	-	2
1908 Cardinals	-	-	-	-	-	10
1961 Athletics	-	-	8	-	*	-
1988 Orioles	-	Worst 1981-90	-	*	*	*

* This year was not included either because it was after the study was published or was arbitrarily excluded by the author.

SOURCES:

HHH - This study.

ROBINSON SALZBERG [SALZ.] - Robinson, George, and Salzberg, Charles. *On a Clear Day They Could See Seventh Place.* New York: Dell Publishing, 1991. They picked the worst team in each decade.

AASENG - Aaseng, Nathan. *Baseball's Worst Teams.* Mankato, Minn.: Lerner Publications, 1984.

MUELLER [MUEL.] - Mueller, Michael. "These Were the Four Worst Teams in the Major Leagues." *Baseball Digest*, March 1983, pp. 44-50.

ALLEN - Allen, Lee. "The Majors' Worst Teams." *Baseball Digest*, February 1951, pp. 5-9.

OLBERMANN [OLBER.] - Olbermann, Keith. "The Ten Worst Teams in Baseball History." *Baseball Quarterly*, October 1979, pp. 61-70.

Our computer found that the 1916 Athletics were the worst team of all time and the other five experts generally agreed that this club was among the worst. One other expert rated them the worst; another, second worst; another, one of the worst four; one rated them third worst and the fifth expert rated them the worst of their decade.

Thus, as with the best team of all time, there was considerable agreement at the "top," but, as with the best teams, agreement was less below that point.

All five of the other studies named one of our computer study's ten worst teams (the 1916 Athletics). Four of the five agreed on two others, two of the five agreed on four others, but no one agreed with us on the teams we ranked seventh, eight and ninth worst.

Of the teams we ranked from 11th through 20th worst, others agreed with us on only two. Of the teams we ranked from 21st to 30th, others agreed with us on three.

The others listed among their worst teams five clubs that did not fall into our Worst 30, but one of them certainly would have been on our list had we included teams from the 19th century.

Four of the five named the 1899 Cleveland Spiders as one of the worst of all and we would have to agree had we included pre-20th century teams. The other four clubs not making our Worst 30 were each named by only one expert.

PART III
TRENDS IN THE
BEST AND WORST

Chapter 23 -
Moving Toward Parity?

As the major leagues have matured, there is far less difference between the best and worst teams. As a result,
in recent years teams have moved from last place in
their division to first place in one year.

Analysis of how the Top 30 and Bottom 30 teams
distribute through the years, as is shown in Table 24
suggests strongly that there has been much more parity
in baseball since World War II.

Table 24
How Top 30 and Bottom 30 Teams
Distribute Through the Years

Time Period	Top 30	%	Bottom 30	%
1901-16	11	34	9	27
1917-18	0	-	0	-
1919-41	9	20	12	26
1942-45	4	50	3	38
1946-93	6	6	6	4
TOTAL	30	16%	30	12%

Note that 11 of the 30 best teams of all time played
before World War I and represent 34% of the 32 pennant winners during that period. While nine teams or
20% of the 46 pennant winners that played between the
two wars were among the 30 best, only six teams or 6%
of the 96 pennant winners that have played since World
War II were among the 30 best.

Conversely, the 30 worst teams of all time distribute in much the same way. Nine played before World War I representing 27% of the last place finishers for that period. Twelve played between the two wars representing 26% of the last place finishers at that time. But only six played since WWII, representing only 4% of the 142 last place finishers (including the last place finishers from both divisions after division play started in 1969).

In other words, the pre-World War I teams were both more likely to be among the 30 best and the 30 worst. It also shows that between the two wars, the likelihood of making both the best *and* the worst list was about the same.

In the 48 years since World War II, 6% of the pennant winners were among the 30 best but only 4% of the tail enders were among the 30 worst, despite the presence of expansion teams.

This shows very clearly that parity among the teams has been much greater since World War II than it was before.

This trend toward parity is normal, according to Stephen J. Gould, who teaches biology, geology and the history of science at Harvard University. He is also an expert on evolutionary processes.

He states that "narrowing variations" is a general property of systems undergoing refinement. In the case of baseball, variations shrink as improvements in play eliminate many inadequacies of the pitchers and players.

Gould says players now are too well trained to permit the extremes of achievement that were true in an earlier time. In the words of George Will, "As baseball has been sharpened - every pitch, swing and hit is charted - its range of tolerance has narrowed, its boundaries have been drawn in and its rough edges smoothed."[1]

The "play" in playing major league baseball is gone, according to Prof. Gould. Baseball has become a science in the sense that it emphasizes repetitious precision in execution of its actions. The variations decrease at both ends with the highest and lowest averages edging toward the league averages.

1.Will, George F.; *Men at Work* (1990: Harper Perennial), page 316+. (Prof. Gould's ideas are also discussed in these pages.)

PHOTO CREDITS

I would like to thank the National Baseball Library & Archive in Cooperstown, New York, for providing the photographs that appear in this book.

ABOUT THE AUTHOR

Harry H. Hollingsworth retired in July of 1982 from the Firestone Tire and Rubber Co. where he had served in managerial positions in sales forecasting, marketing research and strategic planning. One of his first actions after retiring was to buy his own computer.

At Firestone, he had supervised development of computerized models for sales forecasting and inventory control. A lifelong sports fan, he served as sports editor and editor of his high school and college newspapers before earning an MBA at Northwestern University. He has published the *Mathematical Ratings of College Football Teams* since 1982. They have appeared regularly in several newspapers as have his forecasts of college bowl games. He has also forecast NFL game scores and was the *New York Post's* Bettors' Guide champion in both 1991 and 1992.

Hot New Titles of Jewish Interest From S.P.I.

BOOKS

☐ **A Warriors Way: Israel's Most Decorated Commander Relives His Greatest Battles** *by Brigadier General Avigdor Kahalani.* Brigadier General Kahalani not only received the Distinguished Service Medal, but also the Israel Defense Forces' most rarely issued award—the Medal of Valor. In the Six Day War the young tank commander was badly burned when his tank took a direct hit. With charred flesh and his uniform burning he was still barking crucial orders to his men. The battle description is frenzied and detailed as readers are hurled into the history. (ISBN 1-56171-239-6) $5.99 U.S.

☐ **Terrorist's Madonna** *by Elyssa Jordan.* Frank Gabriel is a brilliant American chemist teaching in Chile. His beautiful wife, Rachael, saves him from terrorist kidnappers with ransom money and the only other commodity she had to offer. The trauma pushes Frank to the edge of insanity. In the Arizona desert he meets with a group of world-class scientists who are ready to destroy the world if they can't save it from environmental ruin. Learn how the plot is thwarted and Rachael and Frank find true love.
(ISBN 1-56171-155-1) $5.50 U.S.

☐ **Improve Your Odds Against Cancer: What Everyone Should Know** *by John F. Potter, M.D.* The nationally acclaimed founder of the Vincent Lombardi Cancer Research Center details valuable information on how to protect yourself and those you love against the scourge of Cancer. Dr. Potter's explicit advice includes how to evaluate doctors, early prevention techniques, how to prevent cancer through diet changes, and why most cancers are now curable. "Everything

To order in North America, please sent this coupon to: **S.P.I. Books** •136 W 22nd St. • New York, NY 10011 • Tel: 212/633-2022 • Fax: 212/633-2123

Please send European orders with £ payment to:
Bookpoint Ltd. • 39 Milton Park • Abingdon Oxon OX14 4TD • England • Tel: (0235) 8335001 • Fax: (0235) 861038

Please send ____ books. I have enclosed check or money order for $/£ (please add $1.95 U.S./£ for first book for postage/handling & 50¢/50p. for each additional book). Make dollar checks drawn on U.S. branches payable to **S.P.I. Books**; Sterling checks to **Bookpoint Ltd.** Allow 2 to 3 weeks for delivery.
☐MC ☐ Visa # _____
Exp. date _____
Name _____
Address _____

Great S.P.I Books
Fact And Fiction

☐ **The Super Swindlers: The Incredible Record of America's Greatest Financial Scams** *by Jonathan Kwitney.* They say that crime doesn't pay, but it has paid quite handsomely, thank you, for some of America's greatest swindlers and con-men. Acclaimed investigative journalist Jonathan Kwitney (The *Wall Street Journal, The Kwitney Report*—PBS TV) tracks down these notorious paper pirates who have taken individuals, corporations and governments to the cleaners. In The Super Swindlers we find out how these con-men have been operating and how so many of them have avoided prosecution. (ISBN 1-56171-248-5) $5.99 U.S.

☐ **First Hand Knowledge: How I Participated In The CIA-Mafia Murder of President Kennedy** *by Robert D. Morrow.* We still have far more questions than facts about that dark November day in Dallas. But now out of the shadows, comes the only inner-circle operative not to have been mysteriously assassinated. The author's information was the basis of the House Select committee on Assassinations 1976 investigation. Morrow finally feels the danger to himself and his family passed and he is ready to talk. (ISBN 1-56171-274-4) $5.99 U.S.

☐ **Love Before The Storm: A True Romance Saga in the Shadow Of The Third Reich** *by Roslyn Tanzman.* They were two young Jewish medical students, in love, and studying medicine in Europe's greatest medical schools. The future looked rosy, until the German economy tottered and the right-wing forces marched into power. In this moving, true retelling of her parents' actual love story, Roslyn Tanzman recreates their love at first sight, their class-war between the family and the shadow cast upon the lovers by Hitler's Germany and impending World War.
(ISBN 1-56171-240-X) $5.50 U.S.

Hot Hollywood Titles From S.P.I. Books

SPI
BOOKS

☐ **Sweethearts** The inspiring, heartwarming and surprising stories of the girls America tuned in to watch every week in the 60's these glamorous and sexy stars who made the 1960's a "time to remember" and long for: featuring Goldie Hawn and Judy Carne, Sally Field, Barbara Eden and more. (ISBN 156171-206-X) $5.50 U.S.

☐ **Hollywood Raw** *by Joseph Bauer.* Wouldn't you like to know how **Christina Applegate** and **David Faustino** (Kelly and Bud Bundy on *Married With Children*) live in real life? *Hollywood Raw* also includes informative sections on **Kirstie Alley**, **Rosanna Arquette** and **Arsenio**. Author Joseph Bauer was there on the sets as the studio teacher to the young stars. He saw first hand all the never-reported details of their shocking private lives. (ISBN 1-56171-246-9) $5.50 U.S.

☐ **Who Said That? Outrageous Celebrity Quotes** *by Ronald L. Smith.* Here is the largest collection of memorable quotes from America's top pop icons, stars of the big screen, the small screen, the music scene and more. Readers are challenged to identify the sources of unforgettable quotes. (ISBN 1-56171-228-0) $4.99 U.S.

☐ **Hollywood's Greatest Mysteries** *by John Austin.* Hollywood columnist and author John Austin takes the reader well beyond the prepared and doctored statements of studio publicists to expose omissions and contradictions in Police and coroner's reports. **After** examining these mysterious cases, you will agree that we have not been told the truth about Elvis Presley, Marilyn Monroe, Jean Harlow and others. (ISBN 1-56171-258-2) $5.99 U.S.

To order in North America, please sent this coupon to: **S.P.I. Books** •136 W 22nd St. • New York, NY 10011 • Tel: 212/633-2022 • Fax: 212/633-2123

Please send European orders with £ payment to:
Bookpoint Ltd. • 39 Milton Park • Abingdon Oxon OX14 4TD • England • Tel: (0235) 8335001 • Fax: (0235) 861038

Please send____books. I have enclosed check or money order for $/£
(please add $1.95 U.S./£ for first book for postage/handling & 50¢/50p. for each additional book). Make dollar checks drawn on U.S. branches payable to **S.P.I. Books**; Sterling checks to **Bookpoint Ltd.** Allow 2 to 3 weeks for delivery.
☐MC ☐ Visa # _____
Exp. date _____
Name _____
Address _____

Best Selling Books From
The S.P.I. Catalog